OUR CHILDREN'S FUTURE:

DOES PUBLIC SERVICE MEDIA MATTER?

The Children's Media
FOUNDATION

Our Children's Future: Does Public Service Media Matter?
is a publication of The Children's Media Foundation

Director, Greg Childs
Administrator, Jacqui Wells

The Children's Media Foundation
15 Briarbank Rd
London
W13 0HH

info@thechildrensmediafoundation.org

First published 2021

Book design by Camilla Umar
Cover photo by Efe Kurnaz on Unsplash

ISBN: 978-1-9161353-1-4

The Children's Media
FOUNDATION

CREDITS

Editor ....COLIN WARD

Editorial Team ....ANNA HOME
GREG CHILDS
HELEN MCALEER
JAYNE KIRKHAM
HELEN MCALEER
JEANETTE STEEMERS
JOHN KENT

CMF Executive Group ....AKINDELE AKINSIKU
ALISON STEWART
ANTHONY UTLEY
ASHLEY WOODFALL
CECILIA THWAITES
CHRISTINE SINGER
DIANA HINSHELWOOD
LINCIA DANIEL
MARTIN FRANKS
NIKKI STEARMAN
OLIVIA DICKINSON
ZAINAB BALAM
ZOE MASSEY

Report Design ....CAMILLA UMAR
Web Design ....DAN MOAT, TAHNINIAL

And again, our thanks to all the writers who have given their
time, energy and ideas to this project.

info@thechildrensmediafoundation.org

CONTENTS

Foreword 6
Baroness Floella Benjamin DBE and Julie Elliott MP

Introduction 7
Anna Home

A Message of Support 9
Michael Rosen

Section 1: Is There Any Value in Public Service Media?

Policy, Production and Public Service in the UK – Taking Children Seriously 11
Professor Jeanette Steemers

Here's Not Looking at You, Kids 18
Frank Cottrell-Boyce

Not Waving, But Drowning – An Independent Children's Producer's Perspective 24
Anne Wood

Feeling Included: The Value of Public Service Media 27
Wincie Knight

Time for Another Revolution? 32
Sir Phil Redmond

Education and the Role of Public Service Media 39
John Richmond

Public Service Broadcasting for Children and the Commercial PSBs 46
Emerita Professor Máire Messenger Davies

Section 2: Understanding the Media Experiences of Today's Children

The Physical and the Virtual:
Understanding Children's Relationships with Their Media 53
Anne Longfield

Carrying the Baton: BBC Children's & Education 58
Patricia Hidalgo

Today's Children, Tomorrow's Voters 62
Patrick Barwise and Peter York

Public Service News for Young People: Where Next? 68
Warren Nettleford

Child-Produced Content and the Simulation of Childhood 74
Dr Jane O'Connor

The Appeal of Period Drama for a Younger Audience 81
Dr Shelley Anne Galpin

Why Is Public Service Television for Kids So Important? 87
Nicky Cox MBE and Simona Karabyn

Section 3: Can a New Public Service Media Framework Serve the Children's Audience?

Children's Television: The Canary in the Coal Mine 93
Jackie Edwards

A Global Perspective on Thinking Locally 96
Jenny Buckland

PSM Means 'Personalised Streaming Media'... 99
Timandra Harkness

Why Public Service Media Need to Place Our Trust in the 'Lean In' Generation 104
Japhet Asher

The Active Digital Citizen 108
Lord David Puttnam

Public Service Media: A Matter of Life and Death 113
Dr Mai Elshehaly and Professor Mark Mon-Williams

As Kids Kickstart the Metaverse, Is Public Service Media Ready? 119
David Kleeman

LIKE 129
John Dale

Once Upon a Time, There Was a Broadcaster... Responding to the Distributed
Risk of Children's Programme Production and Consumption 135
Dr Karl Rawstrone

Our Children's Future 142
Ed Vaizey

A Virtuous Circle: Creating a New Additional Funding Model 148
Tom Van Waveren

What Now? What Next? What If...? 153
Greg Childs

Our Writers 161

FOREWORD

BARONESS FLOELLA BENJAMIN DBE AND JULIE ELLIOTT MP

As co-chairs of the All-Party Parliamentary Group for Children's Media and the Arts, we welcome this new campaign by the Children's Media Foundation. Their initiative to commission this series of radical, free-thinking articles will dig deep into the fundamental purpose of public service media content for children and the challenges faced in a media landscape that has changed beyond all recognition.

Over thirty years ago the UK signed up to the United Nations Convention on the Rights of the Child (UNCRC), thus agreeing that children have the right to learn about and practice their own culture, to join in a wide range of recreational activities, and to have access to safe and appropriate mass media. Recent clarification applies the UNCRC to the digital environment as much as the physical world, recognising that for children there is no differentiation: every experience has an impact.

Our children's future is our future. The adults they become and the decisions they make will be the consequences of the childhood we give them now. They don't just learn in formal classrooms: they learn everywhere. So, what they see, hear and experience in the media we give them matters. Will they know enough about the world? Their society, local, national and beyond? Will they care? Will they make it better or worse?

And do we care?

In the past ten years or so, there have been numerous policies dealing with communications and the digital economy, but they have never seen the needs of children as of paramount importance. Even now, Ofcom's public service media consultation, Small Screen: Big Debate, includes very few references to children's content, and the Government's new panel of advisors was initially set up without a single children's specialist. What sort of politics is this? Perhaps that's the problem: public service media is a party-political football rather than a national societal service. It is time to put party aside and put children first with a proper coordinated look at what is best for kids. Because ultimately, what is best for children will be best for us. ◉

Julie Elliott MP & Baroness Floella Benjamin DBE
Co-Chairs APPG for Children's Media and the Arts

INTRODUCTION

ANNA HOME OBE

The Children's Media Foundation was set up to "work towards ensuring that UK kids have the best possible media on all platforms at all ages." Surely not a difficult or controversial ambition, but looking back at our history since 2011, and that of our predecessor, Save Kids TV (2006 - 2011), we still seem to be asking the same questions, focusing on funding, quality, regulation, the future of the BBC, decline in original content; continually facing the same problems without finding satisfactory long-term solutions.

When there are enquiries and consultations about the future of children's media, we always seem to be chasing our tails, trying to catch up, tinkering with the past, defending the status quo.

And here we are again, in 2021, awaiting the outcome of the latest Ofcom consultation on PSB, including children's, and wondering where it will take us.

However, this time the context has changed. The impact of Covid-19 on the whole world and, in CMF terms, particularly on children's lives and media consumption, has made us stop, think and consider whether public service media for kids still really matters and if it does, do we have a unique opportunity to rethink the whole issue and plan a new and different future?

This is why the CMF decided to launch this report.

We asked a wide range of people from inside and outside the world of children's media to consider whether or not they thought PSM for children does still matter and, if so, why and what should be done to move it forward into an exciting, viable future? We asked for articles expressing a range of views from the traditional to the futuristic. We got a terrific, varied and exciting response.

Following the launch of the report at this year's Children's Media Conference, we intend to carry on the debate in the autumn with a series of public online events, which will bring our writers together with policymakers to discuss how some of these ideas might be put into action. We want to make sure the children's audience is not forgotten as government plans the future framework for public service media. We hope when you have read all or some of these articles, you will want to join in the discussion, either by attending these events or by joining the CMF and supporting our work.

This report is not offering one solution; it explores a wide range of different approaches. We see this as the beginning of a process, using a particularly negative event in history to create something positive, by addressing a specific but important aspect of modern children's lives, their media, both what they consume and what they create.

We need to listen not just to the experts and the opinion formers but also to the kids themselves. Kids from different countries and different cultures, many of whom are far ahead of the adults in media terms, and others who struggle with media poverty.

The questions they ask and the solutions they suggest will probably be very different from the ones we have struggled with for so long, but hopefully they may lead us to a new chapter in children's media history, one which embraces the future, but also respects the past.

On behalf of the CMF I would like to thank:

All of the contributors, who have been so enthusiastic and generous with their time.

The editorial team for all their suggestions and constant follow ups.

Our technical support team for designing and running the campaign website.

And especially Colin Ward, the editor of the report, who has done a great job in a very short time, and has, I believe, enjoyed it too!

Thank you all.

Anna Home
Chair The Children's Media Foundation
June, 2021

A MESSAGE OF SUPPORT

MICHAEL ROSEN

Many will know of Michael's ill health. Understandably, he didn't feel up to writing a full article for the campaign but has kindly sent this message of support. As you would expect, it sums up the heart of the argument in just a couple of short paragraphs.

It's all in the name: it's for the public – that's all of us, and it's a service. It serves the people. Children are part of the people, they are people. They are entitled to be given a service that is for all of them. As we become more and more aware of the diverse needs of children (children are diverse), then we need some kind of commitment beyond that of the market to ensure that these diverse needs are served. The market cannot serve this diversity. By definition it has to compete for mass audiences; it has to 'massify' the audiences in order to survive. Of course, public service broadcasting looks to put on popular programmes, but at the same time it builds in a remit to make programmes that express the needs of minorities, who of themselves may or may not be profitable for broadcasters to reach. Further, public service broadcasting can and should see its remit to go beyond broadcasting itself to provide a full range of outreach services and links with other organisations.

Children are themselves treated in our society as a minority. They are often overlooked, marginalised or excluded from decisions even when those decisions affect them directly. This is an outlook, a view or a tendency towards children in society. We are much happier talking about children – as I am here! – than listening to them, or finding ways of expressing their needs, desires and imaginations. Public service broadcasting can, does and should do this. Children are not in the waiting room of life; they are alive, thinking, reflecting, interpreting, re-imagining the world around them. Giving that a voice or seeking to meet those needs with high class, high production values is not necessarily profitable. That's why we need funding for this kind of broadcasting. After all, we don't doubt that spending billions on education is a 'good thing', so why query the 'edutainment/infotainment' principles of public service broadcasting for children?

IS THERE ANY VALUE IN PUBLIC SERVICE MEDIA?

POLICY, PRODUCTION AND PUBLIC SERVICE IN THE UK – TAKING CHILDREN SERIOUSLY

PROFESSOR JEANETTE STEEMERS

One of the most experienced academics working in this field explains why the repeated failure by policymakers to put the children's audience at the heart of public service media is ethically wrong and how government can begin to address this failure.

After the May publication of the damning Dyson Investigation report into the BBC's handling of Martin Bashir's '*Panorama*' interview with Diana, Princess of Wales in 1995, all sides are gearing up for the mid-term review of the BBC's Royal Charter in 2022. It promises to be a bruising encounter. Issues of governance, following a shift towards external regulation of the BBC by UK regulator Ofcom in 2017, might seem tangential to how the BBC serves the UK's children. However, taken as a whole, it all contributes to the slow and steady drip-feed of ideological arguments on three fronts around the future of the BBC, the ethos of public service broadcasting generally, and how public service content should be funded. All three issues are relevant to children and young people, reflecting widely held assumptions about the BBC. As Home Secretary Priti Patel stated in an interview on the BBC's '*Andrew Marr Show*' on May 23, 2021, in response to the Bashir case, "This is the Netflix generation [...] How relevant is the BBC?"

The politicisation of debates around the BBC tend to push any consideration of children's needs to the margins, minimising the Corporation's contributions as a significant curator and funder of UK content for children and young people over many years. Within this febrile atmosphere, the Children's Media Foundation's campaign crucially goes to the crux of the issue, addressing Patel's query directly when it asks whether public service media still matters for children. And unlike other policy consultations, it does put children at the centre of the debate. The CMF's contribution is welcome because it offers a more comprehensive review of issues around content and children's developing experiences, addressing recurring dilemmas about funding, but also pressing for a future vision that extends beyond constantly rehearsed stopgap arguments about broadcast provision by the BBC and commercial PSBs (ITV, Channel 4, Channel 5).

Who is framing the agenda?

One problem which constantly holds back the case for children's public service media is the nature of the policy consultation process, namely – *who gets to frame the agenda, who gets to respond, and who gets listened to*. This has led to plenty of tinkering around the edges in recent years but few interventions that deal with transformations and risk in the children's market. The drawbacks of endless consultations from Ofcom, the DCMS or parliamentary inquiries by the House of Lords and the House of Commons are that matters relating to children are rarely specifically addressed and children are rarely consulted. Consultation responses usually come from the same stakeholders, including children's advocacy groups like the Children's Media Foundation; public service advocacy groups like the Voice of the Listener and Viewer; industry groups like Animation UK, Pact, COBA and broadcasters and other media players, who quite naturally represent their members or business interests rather than children's interests. Most rely on evidence gleaned from Ofcom's annual surveys of public service performance, which year after year show a decline in UK-originated hours (640 hours in 2019 compared to 1584 hours in 2006) and expenditure (from £99m to £79m between 2013-19) on UK children's content by UK PSBs, but rarely reveal much qualitative depth about what parents and children really value about public service content made in the UK, whether they recognise it and whether they want more. What we do know is that a significant minority of children (pp. 20-21 also backed up by YACF research) don't feel that TV shows include people that look like them or represent their localities.

There is also a constant failure to recognise the diversity of children and young people, lumping them all together, when the needs of a 4-year-old are clearly very different from a 10-year-old or a 14-year-old. By contrast, those consultations that do focus on children – for example, Ofcom's Children's Content Review (2017-18) and its 2019 consultation on BBC children's news and first-run UK originations – are either so narrowly drawn that they offer limited scope to move forward or, as was the case with BBC children's news, pre-determined before the consultation was even concluded. The BBC asked for a reduction in originated '*Newsround*' hours from 85 to 35 a year, and Ofcom simply conceded, with little detail about how the BBC intended to cater for children's news and engage them on other platforms.

Tackling inequalities

With all children supposedly able to access boundless services, experiences and content online, this begs the question, **"Why should we care about public service media for children?"** And indeed, there sometimes seems to be an apathy amongst policymakers towards this issue. But these assumptions about children as 'digital natives', who are uniformly engaging with online content and seeking out new experiences, is distorting the policy process. It's true that many children are moving away from linear TV. But these arguments largely ignore deep inequalities in UK society, equalities brought into sharp relief when Covid revealed the extent to which a significant minority of children and families have limited access to electronic devices and wi-fi, let alone Netflix or Disney+, hindering their participation not only in essential education but also essential communication. The pandemic has reminded us of the value of public interventions, the importance of public service values of universal access, quality and diversity, particularly for those children and families who do not have access to the necessities of life, including food but extending to laptops and mobile phones. The BBC showed its worth with initiatives for educational content during the pandemic, but will it continue educational engagement if other more pressing priorities take over?

This isn't an argument for a return to the days of afternoon children's slots on mainstream channels, but it is an argument for the need to recognise that regulated and universal access to information and communications is a child's essential right as laid down in the United Nations Charter on the Rights of the Child. Without regulation and public funding, the market alone is wanting in respect of diverse provision for diverse children, and current debates about online regulation and online harms suggest that similar mistakes are set to be made with little attention paid to positive interventions that ensure public service content is freely available. As Ofcom concludes its Small Screen, Big Debate consultation about the future of public service media, and with the mid-term review of the BBC's Charter next year, there is a danger that children's issues will again drop down the agenda. This needs to be resisted because if we don't engage children and young people in trusted spaces with public service media content and experiences now, then we could be heading for a less cohesive and dysfunctional society further down the road.

Disappointment, again?

In its recent 2021 Small Screen, Big Debate consultation on the future of public service media, Ofcom only mentioned children under 16 infrequently (on 6 pages), and they were not a focus of consultation events. To echo the newly appointed children's commissioner on March 16, 2021: "Society and political structures often short-change children", there is a high risk that policymakers will 'short-change' children again.

Consultation of children, as distinct from undertaking market research in media trackers, has been lacking in previous inquiries. The current Ofcom overview of PSB does not take enough account of the future impact of technological transformations on children's lives or offer to explore their views. Over time this has reinforced an almost laissez-faire approach to children's media and communications needs, which does little to engage with why public service is important for the under-18s, who are marginalised in many other aspects of policy as well. In respect of public service, we only have a partial picture of what they watch, how they find content, and how they interact with it.

The erosion of public service for children since 2003 tells us that arguments in favour of it need to be constantly reformulated and articulated because serving children is often trumped by other short-term considerations – financial and commercial priorities, and more lucrative adult audiences. The current system, of which freely available public service broadcasting is a key part, has contributed to a cohesive democratic society to which children also belong and in which they participate, engage and learn. It underpins children's communications rights, including "access to information and material from a diversity of national and international sources" (Art.17), and the right to require states to give 'due weight' to the views of children, and to provide them with an opportunity 'to be heard' (see UN Convention on the Rights of the Child). Updated in 2021 to take account of children's rights in the digital world, the UN convention underlines that states need to ensure equitable access, that children's rights outweigh commercial interests, and that governments and businesses must take children's views into account, including in matters around the digital world. Current consultations in the UK suggest that this is not happening.

Bring out the public service positives

Ideally, an independent public service for children should include impartial news, educational content, information, drama and entertainment in new formats which reflect the diverse backgrounds of children living in all parts of the UK. It should be universally accessible and easy to find, prominent on any freely available platforms. It should be accessible in a platform-neutral way on-demand and online so that all children can access it. It should be regulated in ways that protect children from harm.

Children's content is part of the UK's overall PSM offer, because commercial providers, many of whom are foreign-owned and minimally regulated, have never supported the full range of UK content that fulfils children's communicative rights in the place where they live. It's disappointing, therefore, that the UK Government's most interesting response to market failure in recent years, namely the establishment in 2019 of the British Film Institute's Young Audience Content Fund (YACF) had its funding cut from £57m to £44.2m in May, leaving £10.7 to spend in its final year.

When the YACF launched it certainly felt like a meaningful positive policy intervention to halt the decline in public service commissioning of UK children's content. Admittedly, the condition of free-to-air distribution has largely limited awards to commissions by commercial PSBs (ITV, Five and Channel 4), in effect a public subsidy, but it has opened opportunities to explore alternative paths with new voices among the production community, to Sky News ('*FYI Investigates with First News*'), and for regional representation and indigenous languages (S4C, BBC Alba). The YACF rekindled investment by commercial PSBs (the BBC did not participate) with the prospect of YACF financial support combined with industry-targeted incentives of tax credits for animation and children's live action. As a different model it does offer a starting point to think about new ways of defining and measuring the value of public service media to children, criteria that are not always open to scrutiny from PSBs. If one key lesson needs to be learned from the YACF, it should be how to extend its effectiveness beyond broadcast-type material largely from mainstream PSBs, to facilitating the distribution and promotion of a wider range of public service material on other platforms.

The Government's decision to cut back on the YACF is indicative of a constant refrain since 2003, when the UK's deregulatory Communications Act removed origination quotas for UK children's content by commercial PSBs (ITV, Channel 4, Channel 5). Restrictions in 2007 on advertising food high in fat, sugar and salt around children's broadcast content led to radical reductions in commissioning, particularly by ITV which had been a key investor in quality UK children's content. The BBC's emergence as the UK's dominant commissioner of children's content arguably proved detrimental for children's choices and the production sector as BBC commissioning declined as part of a 'fewer, bigger, better' initiative after 2007. In hindsight, it's no surprise that children shifted their attention swiftly to online offerings, because PSBs have increasingly failed to provide them with enough of what they really want to watch or engage with. The removal of regulatory quotas and the failure of broadcasters to respond swiftly to new platforms offers a cautionary tale of policymakers failing to provide necessary safeguards, and the uphill battle to win those children back.

What next?

The CMF campaign is keen to establish new future-proof models for public service children's media which will continue to provide children with a rich, diverse range of media experiences that will enhance their lives and address market failure. Looking over the contributions to this submission, several themes emerge on which to build more coherent approaches. They don't provide all the answers, but they offer a start in four key areas that learn from past failings and look further into the future.

BUILD PARTNERSHIPS *WITH* CHILDREN

Public service providers, governments and regulators should be less 'top-down' and work harder to reach out to and engage with young people across the UK. This means more flexibility by the likes of the BBC, Ofcom and others to build collaborative relationships and new definitions of public service across multiple platforms with children and young people, rather than simply deciding for them. It could mean working with other publicly-funded cultural and educational institutions that engage with children – including, crucially, schools and film institutes, as happens in Scandinavia and the Netherlands.

Building partnerships means engaging children and young people seamlessly across the platforms that appeal to them and taking greater account of the significance of gaming, friendship and content creation as markers of their identity, that could contribute to more inclusive definitions of public service. Could public service providers, funders and producers do more to recognise what children and young people can contribute as co-commissioners, co-creators and co-curators, filling the gap between the subscriber, data-driven experiences of Netflix and Disney+ and the unregulated attractions of YouTube? It should mean listening to children, not just about how they create and share content but also about what they value, to ensure that the digital universe is not simply shaped by adults, and that adults take proper account of what different platforms mean to children and what is missing from their media experiences. Respecting and taking children's opinions into account, as ratified by the UN Convention on the Rights of the Child, would go some way to tackling the public service dilemma of not connecting with children on their terms and in the digital world.

INVEST IN MEDIA LITERACY

Closely linked to better partnerships with children in making decisions that affect them is the need to invest in media literacy. As others argue elsewhere, there needs to be improved development of critical digital literacy skills that children need in order to assess what is being reported, how, why and in whose interests to become active, informed citizens in a socially cohesive and tolerant society. This is something which Ofcom has chosen to downplay as part of its statutory duties on media literacy. Yet this is precisely where those entrusted with public service obligations (regulators, broadcasters, funding bodies) can and should exercise leadership, working closely with schools and families to help children navigate the digital space and clearly distinguish between information sources. We know that older children (12-15) trust broadcast news (84%) more than social media (39%) (pp.16-17), and this needs investment to protect that space which represents a core public service priority. This is where regulatory intervention can ensure that children and young people as citizens continue to have access to trusted news and information.

REGULATE FOR DISCOVERY

Policy needs to be more radically focused on where young people access media, making sure there is space for non-commercial content and experiences that are inclusive, diverse and which don't marginalise children in hard-to-reach minority or poorer communities. This means as much emphasis on positive interventions to achieve good outcomes, such as beneficial cultural, social or developmental impacts, as negative regulatory interventions that counter the negative effects of violent, sexual or over-commercialised content. Ideally this should mean prominence for public service content and players on those platforms where screen-based public service content is most easily and frequently accessed and/or watched by children. It means negotiating with commercial providers to ensure that children can easily find it. This will need clear guidance from regulators about how the concept of public service can be reflected, recalibrated and reinvented for social media and algorithmic recommendation. Whereas previous regulatory interventions focused on levels of investment and production quotas, future regulatory work needs to focus much more on how public service content and experiences can be accessed easily and fairly through regulatory interventions around prominence and algorithms.

BEWARE OF UNINTENDED CONSEQUENCES ON FUNDING

Funding public service represents a huge challenge. Public seed-funding for UK content is still a crucial part of today's funding of UK children's content, but it doesn't go far. It is largely locked up in the licence fee, of which the BBC chose to spend £83m (or just over 5%) in 2020 on children's (p. 50) out of £1609m on TV services by genre, and in £57m over three years for the YACF, which was originally top-sliced exceptionally from the licence fee.

As others have argued, this may be time to explore levies on global media companies and platforms who enjoy unparalleled access to UK markets, including production tax credits and low tax rates. But these are powerful companies, backed by a powerful US government hostile to these types of intervention, as other countries have found out. Nevertheless, levies could be used in different ways to support UK-originated children's productions, but also in persuading global players to invest in promotion and discovery through public service algorithms; levies could also make the YACF a permanent fixture.

Alternatives to the licence fee include a household fee (as in Germany), progressive tax-based systems (predominantly in Scandinavia) which involve smaller or larger payments based on personal income, and even collection through utility payments, which dramatically reduced evasion in Italy. All these systems have drawbacks and do not answer the fundamental issue of whether one institution should still receive the bulk of licence fee income, and whether a new approach is needed to serve children and young people across different funders and different platforms, disaggregating children's content from institutions that are finding it harder to reach younger audiences. This could open a new plurality of providers as a truly contestable system, but evidence of how this operates in other countries (e.g., New Zealand) does not necessarily show a better fulfilment of the public service mission for children, and it would require a radical overhaul of the BBC.

Furthermore, for many projects, public funding forms only one part of the budget, and deficit funding from multiple sources means that investment in originations is often shaped by the commercial considerations of others, including international rollouts, which may diminish cultural distinctiveness and also blur public service and commercial priorities. These tensions have been around for many years but are relevant for how publicly-funded or non-commercial public service content can sit comfortably online alongside commercial brands, or whether public service brands need to carve out a distinctive portal or landing page to create a public service space on digital platforms (see David Kleeman's contribution). These are all issues that still need to be addressed, suggesting the future still needs thought from the most important stakeholders: children themselves.

A way forward

The answers to these issues are not straightforward, but a start would be for policymakers in Government and regulatory bodies to sit up, take notice and start to look for solutions that recognise that universal access to quality information and cultural experiences in new formats across multiple platforms is what makes the UK a functioning democracy where everyone, including children, is taken seriously. This is not just an industry issue but also a society issue, where media literate young people contribute to the future stability of a diverse and inclusive democracy; where public service media content and experiences enhance citizenship and active participation, rather than subjecting children to conspiracies, fake news, and hate speech delivered by untransparent algorithms driven by unaccountable digital companies. Yet this requires sustainable regulatory, financial and structural interventions in the digital sphere that allow children to benefit from their communications rights, rather than having those rights curtailed by lack of adult care and communications practices that undermine society. ◯

HERE'S NOT LOOKING AT YOU, KIDS

FRANK COTTRELL-BOYCE

A passionate defence of the importance of children's media to the creative economy and a heartfelt thank you to the people who "create a space where innovation, wildness and fun can flourish".

In his great poem 'The Whitsun Weddings', Philip Larkin describes a whit weekend train trip from Hull to London. Whit was a popular time to get married, so "all down the line fresh couples climbed aboard". From the carriage windows they watch England flashing by. "An Odeon went past, a cooling tower and someone running up to bowl" until they come to London, "its postal districts packed like squares of wheat". The journey is "a frail travelling coincidence". I don't know a better definition of nation than that phrase. And I don't know a better definition of what culture does than Larkin's observation that "all their lives will contain this hour". Shared memories lend the frail travelling coincidence some durability. Of course, shared national memories don't have to come from culture. They can come from sporting triumphs – though they're hard to come by and the follow-up might be 50 years of hurt. They can also come from catastrophes, such as the one we are living through right now.

If we've learnt one thing from the pandemic it is surely that we interpret the world through stories. When it all began we – and I include cabinet ministers and policymakers in that 'we' – we read it through the lens of movies like 'Contagion', in which the thin veneer of civilisation might crack under the strain of shortages and fear, so that we might at any moment start eating each other, or at least start hitting each other with toilet rolls. When that didn't happen, when – on the contrary – we started shopping for our elderly neighbours, putting rainbows in our windows and having socially distanced street parties, we saw ourselves in a kind of reboot of the Blitz spirit. We even found ourselves a hero with unimpeachably World War Two credentials in Captain Tom.

So what story is British television telling our children right now?

We've placed our children under incredible stress. We've asked them to park up their education, their friendships, their social and sporting activities in order to protect the older generation. This is more or less the opposite of the Blitz spirit. Then, children were sent to places of safety while the parents stayed in danger. Now it's the children who are taking the hit in terms of physical and mental health and educational prospects.

Their lives will contain this moment forever and what will it say to them?

Television – or at least a screen – has been an important part of the story. Like many others, my household has for the last year been a frail non-travelling coincidence. Apart from my wife and myself, it comprised a son in his teens who hasn't left home yet, another in his twenties who was about to leave but whose job switched to remote working, and an anxious elderly grandmother who didn't want to be left alone. Shared meals and shared TV turned this ad hoc collection into a household. This has been the case across the country. I asked Twitter if people were watching TV with their kids and, if so, what? If I'd asked about grown-up TV, I could easily have predicted some of the answers. They'd nearly all be from lavishly funded streaming services e.g., 'The Queen's Gambit', 'The Crown' and so on. But when it came to watching TV with children, there was little common ground. Parents were basically curating their own in-house festivals. Someone was watching the entire history of 'Doctor Who' from the very beginning. Another was doing the same with 'The Simpsons'. There are some CBBC programmes; 'Bluey' crops up a lot, as does 'The Next Step' and 'Tracy Beaker'. But 'Cobra Kai' and 'The Mandalorian' are the nearest things to essential viewing. Then, of course, there's Joe Wicks and other good folk making their expertise – whether it was in fitness, cooking or whatever – available to all on YouTube. A lot of children's illustrators and authors did this. I did a lot of it myself.

There's a lot of nostalgia in the programmes those parents listed. I promised myself that I would avoid nostalgia when talking about this. But nostalgia is a way of using the past to hold the present to account, of measuring what we have lost. The children's TV I was privileged to grow up with poured wildly inventive animation, stories from all over the world, aspirational factual programmes and hours of complete silliness into my living room. When years later I worked with Danny Boyle on the opening ceremony of the 2012 Olympic Games, Danny created a montage of all the great TV moments that we thought had gone into creating us, as a kind of thank you to that era.

You could argue, as a lot of powerful people ARE arguing, that those days are gone. The list of content providers I've mentioned – lavish streaming service serials and niche YouTube channels for instance – might provide evidence for that. The BBC should be reduced to its public service core. But a public service stripped down to its merely utilitarian functions is like a country stripped down to its geology. It's not a country anymore. It's just some rocks sticking out of the sea.

First there's the creative argument. The children's TV of my youth was often wildly innovative and inspiring. Often it was most wildly innovative and most inspiring when it was most fully embracing the idea of service. I give you … 'Vision On'. 'Vision On' was designed to give deaf children a chance to enjoy television, but not one moment of the show was pious or worthy. It exploded with unhinged creativity. I'm not using the word 'inspiring' here as a word of praise. I'm using it as a statement of fact. 'Vision On' gave a space – The Gallery – for children to exhibit their own work. It also provided a platform for the nascent Aardman Animations to begin the journey that would lead to Wallace and Grommit. 'Why Don't You Switch Off Your Television Set and Go Do Something Less Boring Instead?' – probably the most public service title ever typed – had the mighty Russell T. Davis on the production team, who went on to re-create 'Doctor Who'. To quote David Sproxton, one of the founders of Aardman, "We were lucky enough to have a small contract with BBC Children's Television, we never imagined our two-man outfit would develop into a major studio of international repute. It's been an extraordinary journey, even if it is one we've taken one frame at a time." This is all before we even begin to talk about how much Harry Potter – now an industry in its own right – owes to 'The Worst Witch'. Or about the fact that when I was watching Brian Cant and Derek Griffiths on 'PlayAway', I was unknowingly listening to the early works of someone who was to become the most influential writer working today: Julia Donaldson.

This kind of alchemical synergy can still happen. One series that did get mentioned a lot on my Twitter feed was 'Ghosts'. 'Ghosts' grew out of that very public service series 'Horrible Histories'. Simon Farnaby, one of the writers and stars of 'Ghosts', went on to work on the Paddington films. Paddington, of course, has his roots in a series of novels, but he gained his furry foothold in the culture step by step, first on 'Jackanory', then an animated series (again, brilliantly innovative with simple puppets against drawn backgrounds) until finally emerging as, I would argue, one of the greatest films of all time. The pop culture sequence I mentioned in the Olympic Opening Ceremony had at its centre an ordinary modern house. I remember one of our government minders voicing concern about this, saying he thought it might look bathetic. He earned a speech from Danny Boyle about how the houses we had grown up in were the crucibles in which the British culture the world adored – from the Beatles, to the Arctic Monkeys, from 'The Forsyte Saga' to 'Doctor Who' – were forged. That sequence celebrates the way TV brought amazing stuff into those houses, and those houses repaid the gift by producing people who would make even more amazing stuff, yay even unto the World Wide Web itself.

Paddington, Doctor Who, Harry Potter, Wallace and Grommit are important components in our economy. Harry Potter alone has generated over £2bn; four times what the fishing industry is worth. But these characters are also a crucial, indelible part of how the world sees us. Over the last few years, I've frequently heard politicians talk about how to teach traditional British values. The argument goes that to have a peaceful and prosperous multi-cultural society, you need a set of values to which every group in that society can subscribe. It's an ambitious project. And the fullest expression of that ambition is … a bit of tinkering with the English and History curriculums and a heated debate about statue-toppling.

You cannot teach values. You can only live them, and by living them share them. As St Francis was fond of saying: teach, teach, teach, and only when all else fails use words. One of the places I found those values when I was growing up was children's TV. It turned its face towards me and said, "This eccentric, inventive, hilarious, good-hearted nation is yours." It is not simply that the people who created Paddington, Doctor Who or Grommit honed their crafts in children's TV. It's that children's TV embodied a set of values that came to their fullest and most forceful expression in those characters. It's why they stand out from the rest.

But that economic and ideological argument is not the most important thing.

The pandemic has been a great moment for television. During lockdowns, households gathered together to watch stuff together just like in the old days of Morecombe and Wise. We all became the Royle Family. This renaissance in viewing has happily coincided with a renaissance in the making of TV drama. Streaming services have supplied hours and hours of lavishly mounted and beautifully produced, frictionless entertainment. I wouldn't have missed 'The Queen's Gambit' or 'Call My Agent' for worlds.

Is there a new children's series that could stand up alongside these? I mentioned before the strong thread of nostalgia running through those tweets about family viewing. What does nostalgia mean here? It means people were able to find and share moments of happiness in a very dark time by reaching back to Mr Benn's house in Festive Road or to the platform of the Llantisilly and Merioneth Steam Traction Company. Nostalgia is a comfort. Are we creating anything now for which our children could reach back to if there are similar dark times in their adult lives? This isn't just a question about the quality of the programmes; it's about where they sit in the schedule, what importance we place on them. It seems to me that when we do produce a cracking children's series like 'Ghosts', it gets rescheduled as a grown-up series. What does that say about us?

It says, "Here's Not Looking at You, Kids"

I am proud to say that I've worked on a big Netflix project and am working on a big Dreamworks project. I'm working with the cleverest, most creative and ambitious people I've ever had the good fortune to meet. But they cannot, *cannot* afford to produce drama that speaks with an accent. I know this because the Dreamworks project I'm working on is based on one of my own books, which was set in Kirkcudbright. Imagine trying to explain how to pronounce that name.

Global studios have to make stuff with global appeal. At its best, that means it has universal appeal. At its worst, it means that it can only make things that are in some way already familiar. It's no coincidence that the biggest international British hits, brilliant though they be, all involve crowns, or at least coronets. We cannot afford to become a nation whose public face is dressing up as characters from its own history – re-enacting our ancient customs for online tourists.

When writers and producers do get a chance to engage with the lives of young audiences, it often works brilliantly. Look at '*Jamie Johnson*' or '*My Mum Tracey Beaker*'. By the way, I'm not at all arguing here exclusively for contemporary realism. The moment when I myself felt most 'seen' (to use a fashionable term) was when an episode of 'The Magic Roundabout' opened with Dougal staring balefully into the camera muttering, "Hello, turned on a bit early for the news have we?" Somehow I found that downbeat cynicism electrifying. As though Dougal had taken the temperature of our living room.

Here's another lesson from the pandemic. That frail, travelling coincidence is frailer than you think. During the insane numbers of hours I spent Zooming and YouTubing to schools this last year, it became very clear to me that many children are not living in that frictionless, super-fast broadband Netflix world. In any session, I would find kids desperately trying to stay on board using phones and data. The stories they wrote pulsed with anxiety and isolation.

Stories abhor a vacuum. If we vacate the storytellers' chair by the campfire, another storyteller will take our place. If we don't tell our own stories, someone else will tell theirs. And their story may well not be 'The Saga of Noggin the Nog'. It may well be a story about how democracy is pointless because all governments are corrupt. It may be a story about how medical science is really a conspiracy bent on delivering the sheeple into the hands of paedophile owl-worshipping globalists. We are living through a moment of almost unprecedented fury. Everything divides us. Brexit or Remain. Mask or No Mask. Meghan or Kate. Every new story is savagely sliced into a binary choice. This is what happens when you abandon the anxious and the isolated to the market.

Our children's lives will contain the Covid-19 moment forever. Will they remember that the generations who had found wonderland at the bottom of the rabbit hole abandoned them to a warren of darker, depressing rabbit holes on YouTube?

I said that we are the stories we tell. But the truth is we become the stories we tell. The story we seem to be telling at the moment is that children and young people should be seen in the John Lewis advert. But not heard. People who are not heard always do make themselves heard in the end. And when they do, they won't be quoting Paddington's Aunt Lucy, "If we're kind and polite the world will be right."

The spirit of eccentricity and innovation, that love of the detail of our lives and rhythms of speech that was there in Oliver Postgate or 'Grange Hill' still illuminates shows like the wonderful 'Bluey', and in 'Tracy Beaker'. But I get the feeling these are the flowers that have wiggled their way through the concrete of institutional indifference and defeatism. The response to the big-budget behemoths of the streaming services cannot be defeat and retreat. "Nothing ever stands still," said Orwell in his essay, 'The Lion and the Unicorn'. "We must add to our heritage or lose it, we must grow greater or grow less, we must go forward or backward." I still believe we can go forward with Bluey, Tracy, Charlie and Lola and the rest. We can – we must – create a space where innovation, wildness and fun can flourish without immediately being diced and sliced by the market.

We need to take children's TV seriously. Because nothing is more serious than our children.

When Larkin's train finally got to Kings Cross (the station from which Harry Potter left for Hogwarts) he says:

"As the tightened brakes took hold, there swelled
A sense of falling, like an arrow-shower

Sent out of sight, somewhere becoming rain."
Julia Donaldson, Michael Bond, Tony Hart, Biddy Baxter, Joy Whitby, Anna Home, Molly Cox, Eric Thompson, Gordon Murray, Alison Prince and a host of others, we were your arrows. Thank you for our flight.

Let us find a little plot of soil to nourish when we fall as rain.

NOT WAVING, BUT DROWNING - AN INDEPENDENT CHILDREN'S PRODUCER'S PERSPECTIVE

ANNE WOOD

From one of our most respected producers, a call for Government to recognise the production sector faces an almost impossible situation and is rapidly losing the talent and specialist expertise to serve the needs of UK children.

Once upon a time in the United Kingdom every broadcaster originated children's programmes. It was an accepted requirement, integral to the privilege of broadcasting. It was built into the BBC Charter from the beginning. Children's culture was recognised and perceived as important. This premise was consequently also adopted by the ITV companies. The then Independent Broadcasting Authority took a keen and serious interest to ensure that homegrown children's programmes were delivered.

In April 2021 when Ofcom examined children's viewing habits during lockdown, the headline was: "Traditional TV a turn-off as children switch on to YouTube and Netflix". UK children's television was presented as quaint and as antiquated as videos; eliminated by technological change.

This perception began as long ago as 1988, when children's programmes were abolished from Channel 4.

For a time, between 1993 and 2002, when CBeebies and CBBC channels were set up, the regulating authority offered some protection. Then, in 2003, Ofcom was established to assess whether the public service broadcasters, taken together, transmitted a suitable range of high quality programmes for children and young people. With no individual responsibility, ITV companies could begin to withdraw. In 2006, Ofcom published details of restrictions intended to limit children's exposure to advertising of food and drink products high in fats, salt and sugar. "Alas," wailed the companies, "this means we can no longer afford to continue the expensive business of originating new children's programmes." Further funding was withdrawn.

For a time, sales of ancillary products filled the funding gap, but this, too, soon failed. The subtle, and not so subtle, shift to programmes that could be merchandised ended abruptly. Toys "R" Us finally collapsed in 2018.

In 2003, the Communications Act made originating new children's programmes non-essential for ITV. The interests of broadcasters were paramount. At one blow, the internal market for children's programme-making virtually disappeared. Once the competition from ITV was removed, the BBC was the only independent customer remaining. International buyers look first to a programme's success in its home territory, but with only one real UK destination, there was effectively no home market.

The removal of competition was not good for the BBC; it was not good for programme-making and it was especially not good for children's television culture. This is the cold, hard world of money.

There is a belief among those who deal in money for its own sake that the market always adjusts itself. We in the British children's television production business have no market and, consequently, we have no money.

Those of us who have campaigned for years to address these inequalities had a small success in engineering the Young Audiences Content Fund, now nearing its end. Broadcasters, for the most part, including the BBC, closed ranks against it. They, and we, knew that the money would soon run out. £60million, welcome though it was, was never going to close the funding gap. For comparison, consider that in 2005 one series of 'In the Night Garden' cost £14 million.

'In the Night Garden', very successful though it still is in the UK, never achieved the international success of the 'Teletubbies'. 'In the Night Garden' is more firmly rooted in the culture of nursery rhymes. It refers not to a computer generated universe but the gentle woodland world of so many bedtime stories. It belongs to the same storytelling culture and is equally highly valued in countless UK households with young children. This cultural issue is important.

There will never be another 'In the Night Garden'. This is not because there is not the talent to create one, but because we are now in a place where there can never be the money. Lacking opportunity, the talent will wither and potentially die.

How can children not enjoy the glitz and glory of the skilled North American giants? They already pick up its language and absorb the fantasy. Why should they not? These networks have instant global reach, the same content for all children no matter where they live. The media landscape has changed and it will go on changing, but underneath it all, children's own perceptions remain the same. They also need to recognise reflections of their own experiences. They need, as one child put it, stories to make them "feel good inside".

'Teletubbies' briefly demonstrated that we can compete, but that was long ago and far away, before the transition to brave new technology. Imagine trying to sell the 'Teletubbies' concept to any of today's big competitors! Live-action teddy bears with screens in their bellies and antennae on their heads living far away in a dome in a field? What does any of it mean? It is, in fact, a conversation with young children themselves, from their point of view. It succeeded the world over. It was not done to reassure adults or funders. It was done to make children smile. It had the combined funding support of BBC Children's, BBC Education and BBC Worldwide, but its overnight success was due to 12 years' previous experience of making programmes for ITV and observing children's responses to them. There was a belief that quirky and eccentric though it seemed, it was embedded in an understanding of the internal lives of young children.

Over the centuries, ideas of childhood have changed. Medieval society absorbed children invisibly into the adult world. Victorian society sentimentalised them. Early 20th-Century society urged them to higher things. Our century once more treats them as mini adults.

In the UK, children's programme-making has been allowed to become niche. As this is written, in the first week of May 2021, across all available children's channels, excluding the BBC, animation (particularly North American animation) dominates. At the BBC there is a dilution of live action UK drama in favour of reality shows, frequently aping adult television. For younger children especially, there is a crowding of four- and five-minute animated episodes.

Another headline from April 21st this year quotes, "Children rediscover the joy of reading during lockdown"; of course they did. They had more time and, just possibly, a surfeit of similar continuous programming from the small screen had failed to fully satisfy them. Left to themselves, children will always find new alternatives, which is why it is so important that there should be diverse television alternatives for them to discover.

Lack of money is crucial to the demise of the independent children's television sector, but at the heart of the problem lies a deep cultural issue that needs to be addressed. Other nations have systems for safeguarding the equal rights of children to access indigenous work. In the UK, children's programme production is tolerated only on the most minimal terms. The whole infrastructure that supported a thriving, internationally successful children's production sector has been dismantled and displaced.

Casting around for solutions, it is easy to find disadvantages with quotas with sponsorship with regional funding. It is unlikely a fairy godparent will appear to address this situation. We must make our own happy ending, but we can only win if there is a level playing field. We can only win if children's shifting television culture is acknowledged. Government intervention is not a popular idea, but when the picture is one of increasing desperation, what are the options?

Unless securely funded competition within the home market is restored, innovation will fade away, the UK's place at the cutting edge of the children's television industry will never be regained, and children will never have known a difference. ⊙

FEELING INCLUDED: THE VALUE OF PUBLIC SERVICE MEDIA

WINCIE KNIGHT

An incisive reflection on the lasting impact the children's media industry can have on young people and how that privilege and power can be used to give every child a sense of belonging and show them they can be whatever they want to be.

Today's children are tomorrow's adults. That sounds like a truism, but actually it's a simple and important fact that we all occasionally forget. What our children see, hear and experience today will impact the way they act and the decisions they take in the future. Once you understand this as a broadcaster, producer or writer, you can't ignore the great power and responsibilities that creating content for kids implies.

> *I believe the children are our future*
> *Teach them well and let them lead the way*
> *Show them all the beauty they possess inside*
> *Give them a sense of pride to make it easier*
> *Let the children's laughter remind us how we used to be*

These are inspirational words from one of my favourite songs 'The Greatest Love of All', sung by Whitney Houston. It always makes me feel emotional because inclusion is about a feeling, and the powerful feeling of inclusion can never be underestimated. And Whitney is right: we need to be reminded of what it is like to be a child in an adult's world. Life for children today is very different to what we experienced during our own childhoods, so we can't guess what they want, but we can help make them feel happy, proud, safe and included.

Children's media has the opportunity and responsibility to role-model inclusion. The cultural anthropologist Margaret Mead said, "Children must be taught how to think, not what to think." Children should be woven into the fabric of children's media, and it is imperative for inclusivity to be encouraged and practiced in children's media strategies. Everyone digests media differently, and being able to cater your message to diverse audiences will help connect and educate all audiences. Understanding the importance of inclusivity, and the value of knowing your audience, will help shape the way children's media make content relevant. As Barack Obama said in his 2008 campaign, "Yes; we can" be and *stay* relevant.

In order to keep children's media relevant and appealing to today's kids, we need to put them at the centre of these discussions. We must ask them what they need and want to see on screen and, more importantly, what is missing. If we let children lead the way with inclusive practices, the kids' media industry will naturally future-proof itself, staying relevant to the audience and creating a sense of belonging for all viewers. I am hopeful that the ongoing policy review into public service media by Ofcom and the DCMS will similarly seek to put children at the heart of their thinking as they deliberate policy interventions that will shape media regulation for the next decade.

As a parent, I believe it is always important to listen to my children. I particularly hate the old-school saying that "children should be seen and not heard". I believe, children should be seen and heard, as they have a lot to say and are very in tune with what is happening around them. As broadcasters and content creators, we have the power to make this happen. In order to bring children's voices to my article, I asked my own children why we should care about children's media and why it is important. They were very clear in their answers: **"Because content is important to us, to kill boredom"**, **"because we need to hear stories about ourselves that are relatable"**, **"because TV is not just for adults, we are important too"** and **"technology is the new way to watch whatever you want whenever you want"**. They have obviously been around my Zoom calls talking about inclusion whilst homeschooling.

In essence, kids need content tailored for them: that message is pretty clear. They need to see themselves reflected on TV, and technology means they are used to watching what they want, whenever they want it (almost). Children are a very discerning audience and the children's media industry cannot afford to rest on its laurels. Listening to today's children and their needs is essential if we want to move forward and still be the destination kids choose to watch their favourite content.

But let's go back to 1990. Yes, let's go back to the 90's when '*The Simpsons*' first aired, '*Home Alone*' was first released, Tim Berners-Lee published a formal proposal for the World Wide Web, and Nickelodeon, as part of the opening of the Nickelodeon Studios, unveiled the Nickelodeon's Declaration of Kids' Rights, a very important document that was inspired by the USA's Bill of Rights and is still used by the network internationally. This declaration states:

> You have the right to be seen, heard and respected as a citizen of the world.
> You have the right to a world that is peaceful.
> You have the right to be treated with equality regardless of the colour of your skin.
> You have the right to be protected from harm, injustice and hatred.

You have the right to an education that prepares you to run the world.

You have the right to your opinions and feelings, even if others don't agree with them.

Nickelodeon shared these rights because they supported and believed in justice, equality and human rights *for all kids*. I believe the Nickelodeon bill of rights is as powerful and relevant today as it was 31 years ago. It shows that inclusion has always been in the DNA of ViacomCBS, and it has stood the test of time.

Nickelodeon's motto has always been to listen to the audience and put them first in everything we do. Kids' content creators and broadcasters need to listen to kids now more than ever. If you want to make content for children, who are the purest and most honest audience you will ever find, listen to them and go find their voices. They will tell you exactly what they want. Oliver Wendell Holmes states, "Pretty much all the honest truth telling there is in the world is done by children." Listening is a good step in the right direction to creating authentic, inclusive content.

A good example of a show which listens to children and includes their voices is Grandpa Productions' '*The World According to Grandpa*' which airs on Channel 5's kids' block, Milkshake! The show is a humorous, imaginative, creative storytelling format designed to inspire children to laugh and learn through relatable intergenerational relationships. The beauty of the show is that each of the 25 episodes is prompted by a question posed by one of the three grandchildren. Children's voices are well and truly embedded in the show as the questions asked of grandpa are genuine questions asked by children, which were gathered from numerous visits to schools by the writers. Real kids with real and relevant questions.

If you want to make content for children, you need to listen to kids, but not just any kids. You need to listen to a diversity of children's voices and experiences. Content creators should always ask themselves: "Whose voice is missing? How are you going to access real authentic kid's voices and experiences? Are you making content for yourself, out of nostalgia from when you were young, or are you making content for a new generation that is hungry to see themselves and their lives reflected on TV?"

"The best way to make children good is to make them happy." Oscar Wilde

The world is changing fast and the children's media industry has the privilege and great responsibility to be a window to the world for kids. Messages of inclusivity, kindness, honesty and empathy, if embedded into children's media the right way, can have a long-lasting impact on children and their future. Business leaders are currently embarking on training, learning to be inclusive leaders and educating themselves on diversity, equity and inclusion. It's a brilliant thing to see adults getting involved and learning, although perhaps these qualities should be taught at an earlier age? We can't predict what the future holds, but inclusion will always be valuable in a world that is forever changing, and we need to equip children to embrace differences. Also, if diversity on screen is paramount, the best way to tell authentic, diverse stories is to have diversity off screen as well.

The media industry holds great power over the socialisation of children. Do we want children to feel included or excluded when engaging with content? Children's media has the power to influence viewers in many positive ways, but this can also become problematic if underrepresentation and exclusion or negative portrayal and stereotypes of certain identities (such as gender, race, disability and socioeconomic diversity) are not considered. Research shows that a lack of representation in media can lead to negative psychological outcomes for those with identities that are underrepresented or negatively portrayed (Tukachinsky, Mastro, & Yarchi, 2017). **The pain of exclusion is real.** Psychologists believe that it is important for humans to feel a sense of belonging, and at ViacomCBS, we use a strapline when talking about inclusion: "Be You, Belong". Everyone wants to feel included, and the business case for inclusion is overwhelming, especially in the creative sector.

Why would you not want different perspectives, different stories, different voices and experiences to influence your content? It makes for more interesting viewing. Children need to be entertained and educated about the world. Diversity in children's media can and should open children's minds to be the next content creators. There is a saying that "you can't be what you can't see", so let's start role modelling so that children's minds are open and not restricted.

All children need to be seen and heard so that they can aspire to their dreams. Children's media can help children believe that the Nickelodeon bill of rights is achievable. We are missing a trick if we don't give children a voice.

The artist Nas, who recently won a Grammy, recorded a song a few years ago which amplified through the voice of children the lyrics: "I know I can, be what I want to be, if I work hard at it, I will be where I want to be." Those lyrics give voice to that right; children deserve the chance to be what they want to be without restrictions or low expectations because of their background, race or religion, similar to the Nickelodeon bill of rights. Representation in children's media is key, hence why **Children's media is necessary, as it shapes the future of tomorrow's adults.** All children should be taught that they can be whatever they want to be.

Nickelodeon has a history of consciously defying the conventional wisdom with the kinds of characters and stories it captures and represents in its shows: a Latina heroine ('*Dora the Explorer*'), a biracial princess and knight ('*Nella the Princess Knight*'), a Black April O'Neil ('*Rise of the Teenage Mutant Ninja Turtles*'), a diverse foster family ('*Hunter Street*'), a girl quarterback ('*Bella and the Bulldogs*'), a big family of 11 siblings with same-sex parents ('*The Loud House*'). More recently, there has been a show centred on a Latina family, including a kid with Down Syndrome ('*The Casagrandes*'), a disabled pup ('*PAW Patrol*'), kids of Indian heritage ('*The Twisted Timeline of Sammy & Raj*').

The media has a duty to reflect the world and celebrate differences. "There can be no keener revelation of a society's soul than the way in which it treats its children," said Nelson Mandela.

We have talked about the changing world; we need to discuss how children place great value in our world. Equity and sustainability are things children want to champion and they are passionate about it. How do we mix the world of influencers, who children look up to, with the world of children's public service media? '*Go Green with the Grimwades*' does just that. A factual entertainment, reality-based environmental show, it was commissioned from Dochearts, a BAME-owned production company, with financial support from the Government's Young Audiences Content Fund (YACF), which is administered by the British Film Institute.

The Grimwades are a famous YouTube family consisting of mum, dad and their six homeschooled children, who have over 32 million channel views and 254,000 subscribers. The show helps viewers learn to be more environmentally conscious with the five R's: Reduce, Recycle, Repair, Reuse and Refuse. This Milkshake! show educates children on topics such as plastic awareness, using water efficiently, connecting with nature, reusing clothes and the benefits of a zero-waste household. The show also embeds soft learning on numeracy, literacy, and STEM. Learning through entertainment equals edutainment. In order to stay relevant, children's media needs to research all the platforms where children are finding their content. My children love their Nintendo Switch and playing Roblox (safely). Children's media producers need to understand what makes children tick in order to offer them what they are looking for.

It's been a tough year for all of us, especially for children. Children's media has been important in providing a source of escapism for kids. We have learnt from Covid-19 that we can still do things efficiently and successfully through remote working.

I believe that bringing together the creativity of young minds with our more seasoned and experienced content producers is the way forward. My favourite quote is this: "You don't know what you don't know until you don't know it." In the spirit of inclusion, bring different voices into the room and listen.

TIME FOR ANOTHER REVOLUTION?

SIR PHIL REDMOND

A timely reminder as to why we should care about public service media for children, as well as some radical ideas on how we can meet the challenge.

It feels odd, having created 'Grange Hill' and watched it run for 35 years, that there appears a need to even ask if children's media content is worth preserving. Is that not a question containing its own answer, illustrated by our rich heritage of output?

A heritage that stretches back to BBC Radio's 'Listen with Mother' in 1950 and follows a commonality across subsequent generations and technology platforms, to offer quality content to our children. Content that also provides parents with a welcome diversion. A safe space that will occupy children, even keep them quiet every now and then, and, hopefully, be educational, while parents can get on with other things, secure in the knowledge that the electronic babysitter has been vetted, is safe and will not lead their offspring astray. Something that has been amplified across the pandemic.

The fact that DCMS has provided funding to the Young Audiences Content Fund also suggests that the principle is still accepted, even though the mechanism of delivery has become unclear. And that, perhaps, is the most pertinent point. Why, or how, did we get to this point of doubt?

The answer to that is embedded in the British system of revolution: to make great structural change, then have the debate about what we really meant to achieve. It is why we are still debating the 1870 Education Act, which established the principle of state education but never settled the argument about what sort of education. And why, despite the blueprint drawn by the 1942 Beveridge Report, we still do not have a coherent framework for welfare and social care.

Public service media for children fits neatly into this milieu, recognising that it is a surrogate for the future of public service broadcasting as a whole. The two are inseparable, because without the latter, the former would not exist. It was the publicly funded BBC that pioneered the concept, with ITV forced to follow as part of their public service obligations, or price, for being given a monopoly on television advertising in the 1950s.

And for a time, between the 1960 and 1980's, a typically British compromise worked, and children in particular were well-served with strong programming across the schedules. It also worked because of the technological limitations of transmission. A transmitter pattern set out in the 1920s for radio only provided scope for two national television channels, making entry difficult but regulatory control relatively easy.

As technology marched on and brought the potential for more channels and greater competition, regulation became more complicated and in the quest to retain a balanced ecology, every other commercial broadcaster also had to accept public service conditions, including programming for children, while the BBC was encouraged to become more commercial. But not too much.

Gradually, throughout the 1980 and 90's, with ITV's monopoly on advertising slowly eroding, the obvious compromise was to start easing their onerous public service remit, just as questions started to emerge about the purpose of the BBC itself. With new entrants like Sky and Channels 4 and 5, often staffed with ex-BBC people, the purpose of the BBC itself came under scrutiny along with whether the licence fee, another 1920s legacy, was still justified and/or for use solely by the BBC. And within this recurring debate about regulation one question seemed to go unasked. How many public service providers do we really need?

That question is not about how many entertainment platforms we need but, in the age of concern about fake news, cyber bullying, grooming, scamming and the digital divide, more a cultural question of whether we, as a society, want and are prepared to fund a curated, trusted safe space for our children's consumption.

To the British revolutionaries that in itself may sound too radical, but before they knee-jerk and reach too quickly for the concept of plurality, the euphemism for competition, let's just pause for a moment and focus on what we mean by public service. We do not hear clamours for plurality in health, education or policing, so in a digital age when access to broadband is now being considered on a par to other utilities, should we not also consider public service content in a similar light, linked and more integrated with other public services?

If this last year has taught us anything, it is the need for public funding where and when necessary, the need for accurate and well-informed information, and that plurality and competition can also be about harvesting best practice rather than driving out competitors. From history, we know the birth of another great British institution, 'The Archers', came from a union between the Department of Agriculture and the BBC. This is not something to be shied away from, especially as the combined media budgets of the major Whitehall departments probably match, or even eclipse, the terrestrial programme production budgets.

From my own experience, with 35 years of 'Grange Hill', 21 years of 'Brookside', and 'Hollyoaks' still running, I learned that one of the best resources available to contemporary storytellers is a good relationship with other public services. We are all in the births, deaths and marriages game, with a bit of crime thrown in.

Each year, before sitting down to write the overall storyline for 'Grange Hill', I would talk to educators, teachers and pupils. I would criss-cross the country, visiting schools, comprehensive to public, urban, suburban and rural, ostensibly to talk about what it was like to write for television, and during the Q & As I would ask them, initially, what they wanted to see on screen, then, as things progressed, what we were getting right or wrong. If I heard the same tales on the majority of visits, it meant they were of general concern and, as such, relevant areas for drama. The perennial frustrations over school uniforms, homework, hating sports, bullying and, occasionally, their favourite and not-so favourite teachers, but amongst the feedback were always issues like discrimination, inequality and, of course, social justice. Especially that wonderfully coherent youthful sense of right and wrong. Black and white. Something all children are born with.

Why could boys do such and such and girls could not? And, vice versa. Why do teachers use humiliation as a control mechanism? Why can't girls wear trousers? That wasn't a vice versa issue, but another common issue was representation. Why couldn't they have a say in how their schools were run? That one went straight into Series 2 and was one of the early controversies that, with hindsight, helped propel the show to its later campaigning success when some of those who had been first in to criticise it as a work of subversion realised, perhaps like their predecessors at the Dept of Agriculture, that it was reaching the very children they themselves were failing to reach. It was, actually, in the Reithian tradition to inform, educate and entertain.

That took a few years, and the support, courage and commitment of the BBC Children's Department and, in particular, the then Executive Producer of Drama, CMF Chair Anna Home, to reach that point, but it was a journey fortified by the growing audience appreciation.

Within that is another important point. It is often not about systems but people and their willingness to back their own hunches and make the system work. It is about creating a secure environment in which they can operate. Although meeting Anna was one of those right moment, right time, right idea convergences, to get there I had also criss-crossed the country trying to convince one of the big five regional ITV companies that made children's programming that a drama about school was a good idea. All five immediately rejected it. Why would kids want to watch something about school after being there all day? They completely missed the point: because it was relevant to *their* world.

Of course, several years later, after the success of 'Grange Hill' was obvious, the ad-sales folk at ITV tried to persuade me to switch, but by then I knew I would never have been given the same level of commitment, or longevity, as the BBC. For them, and me, it would have been a short-term gain but without the true public service remit, rather than their piecemeal, perhaps burdensome licensing obligation, there would have been too many pressures to compromise. Advertisers were far less forgiving back then.

That is not to do a disservice to advertiser-funded programming, more a recognition of the ingenuity that went into constructing a system to manage the scarce public airwaves that allowed a balanced ecosystem to evolve. The BBC, across its by-then two channels, more than covered the 'inform and educate' parts of the Reithian public service mantra, while ITV, with its Theatre, Cinema and Bingo Hall founders, settled more at the entertainment end. Each pushed and fed off each other. Talent, new blood and ideas easily flowed back and forth. ITV matched and often pushed the BBC into areas like animation, local drama with regional accents, and Saturday morning scheduling (another godsend to every parent).

Recognising and appreciating this balance was another important step in my empirical journey. That to make a real difference, to make a meaningful contribution to social debates, there are three imperatives. Trust, scale and longevity. Each builds on the others. 'Grange Hill' could only have achieved the heights it did at the BBC. The BBC Children's Department had the scale to imbue a philosophy in its staff, it already had the trust of the nation and, most importantly, it had a distant horizon. Because of all three it could afford to take risks, as well as taking the time to fine tune and get things right. In thinking on the future of children's content, size matters.

The best example of how all this can come together was the Zammo drugs storyline. To portray this issue properly it was set over two years, Series 9 and 10: one year to show the dangers and descent into drugs, the next to illustrate a path to recovery. The programme worked with SCODA (Standing Committee on Drug Abuse) and eventually co-operated with the global Just Say No Campaign, something that took the cast to meet Nancy Reagan in the White House. Something that would probably be more feted today in the new era of projecting Britain's soft cultural power.

On the first point, I believe the answer is yes. There is both a demand and room for another long-running contemporary drama for the 'Grange Hill' age range of 8-16. All the usual rites of passages still exist, even if they are reinterpreted as cyber bullying, sexting, ghosting or grooming. Zammo's storyline helped to change the way people viewed drug abuse, more as a social consequence than criminal delinquency, one leading to the other. Imagine the possibilities of being plugged into the Twittersphere.

And yet. And yet. It is all very well knowing what is a good thing. The question of *how* remains. That inevitably takes us to the money and, more importantly, where does it come from and how can it be sustained? The DCMS fund is a welcome intervention, but through the application criteria it is clearly a subsidy for the existing broadcasters and, at £57m over three years, nowhere near enough. In either cash or time.

From my own journey, you can be forgiven for thinking I would like to return to some nostalgic golden age. But that would be wrong. All golden ages are only the ones you worked through. And just as Grange Hill's first-year intake graduated and were replaced by a new cohort, so each generation finds its own touchstones. What worked back then would not work now. We no longer have a balanced and easily controlled regulatory framework. There is no such thing as territory in the digital universe, with VPNs making national boundaries ever more porous. But we should learn from history. The challenge ahead is not about controlling accessibility but exploring the point those five ITV companies missed with 'Grange Hill': relevancy.

The challenge is to provide a safe and trusted, curated destination. That challenge stretches beyond the BBC to both the secondary public service broadcaster, Channel 4, and the commercial licenced services, but it is not about them per se. Who sits where and when. The real debate is what to do with the public's willingness to still provide the greatest tool we have for social intervention. A willingness to provide the revenue. Overall, it is about the cultural compact through which the public still considers it a 'good thing' to fund public service content. Our two main public service providers, BBC and Channel 4, are licensed to collect c£4.5bn per year. The most pertinent question is what, collectively, do we want to do with that level of cultural funding in the future?

Having made the point about scale, reach and longevity, the BBC is an obvious place to start, but it should not be a simplistic demand that it does more, or less, of everything. It is time, coming up to its own centenary when we need to take a look back and ask if it is a good thing worth preserving, and if so, if we were starting again, what would we want it to do, whether the Reithian refrain is still valid, and how should we fund it?

My guess, in the post-Covid world, would be to keep two out of the three, but accept that the third, 'entertain', needs closer scrutiny. Not due, as we constantly hear, to the threat from Netflix, Amazon Video, Disney et al, for they are not competitors to our public service broadcasters. They are the disruptors of the film industry. Streaming is not the threat, it is only a tool, like the BBC iPlayer.

So, if we were starting again, we would probably want our publicly-funded media providers to do what has been asked of the BBC since the 1920s, and Channel 4 nearly four decades ago: promote our shared cultural values, history and, by being more diverse, look for the current gaps and unheard voices. This has often been referred to as the 'market failure model', but television has never really been a true market. Merely a controlled space. The real model, actually, is public service social intervention. Public health, clean water, policing, fire and rescue were not the result of market failure but clearly needed social interventions. Is not a safe, well-curated and trusted space for children's media content equally important?

I would suggest we would start with a new mantra: inform, educate and innovate. '*Listen with Mother*', '*Blue Peter*' and '*Grange Hill*' were innovative at the BBC. As '*Tiswas*' and '*Rainbow*' on ITV and much of Channel 4, including '*Brookside*', of course. So, a key part of redefining what we should expect from our public service providers would be innovation, constantly searching for new ideas, new people, new ways of doing things. In many ways, public service media gives us the creative development lab through which people and ideas develop, but are free to blossom commercially, while the publicly funded lab retains an interest in the IP guaranteeing a return on its investment. How to Bake Off while holding on to the recipe. A way of having our cake and eating it, perhaps.

Nor would we now think of a new, specific tax for funding. It was the only mechanism available in the 1920s, and now, a century later, it feels and is anachronistic. In today's digital environment we would probably go to something like VAT, collected at the point of purchase and remitted to government. Why not then consider adding something to every phone and broadband contract? Just like the additional costs added to our community charges to fund non-council public services, like the police or fire and rescue, why not add a 'cultural precept' to every phone bill?

According to the ONS, 95% of homes have a TV Licence, exactly the same number of homes that have mobile phones. Yet there are around 79 million mobile phone contracts. A cultural precept of £60 a year on each would provide the same level of funding as the current BBC licence fee, without all the issues around criminality, over-75s, hotels and hospital pricing, or costs of collection. So, why not a quid or two to fund children's content?

Then there is Channel 4, currently licenced to collect around £1bn in revenue. After 40 years, I would suggest that its original remit of providing a platform for those unheard voices and independent production has been a resounding success, but perhaps now is also time to reconsider which diverse voices are not being heard properly. Is there not an argument for looking at whether we need Channel 4 as a stand-alone public service provider anymore, or could it be merged into a new, singular, redefined public service content provider, with its £1bn revenue, or a substantial part of it, going toward children's media content?

Across the landscape, the commercial broadcasters should be unshackled from pretending to be part of the full public service mantra, returning to their roots as purveyors of indigenous live-action entertainment, cut free to maximise commercial opportunities, while removing the fears and opprobrium around advertising and sponsorship. No child reaches school without years of bombardment by well-intentioned publishers of educational content or manufacturers of educational toys. Indeed, no child even gets home without the intervention of the clothing and feeding industries. Fast food may be off limits, but what about the nappy manufacturers and pedlars of soothing creams? It is at the parents, not the children, that such advertising and sponsorship can be aimed.

Of course, a review on this scale will face challenges, not least from those reaching for the little bit pregnant cliché, for that is what it is. It is also, well, not just passé but daft. No one seems to worry about institutions like The Guardian, FT or the Economist being tainted by taking advertisements. Indeed, the Scott Trust model for The Guardian, where its commercial interests underpin the survival of the newspaper, is worthy of comparison.

In summary then, the answer to the question of whether public service content for children should be protected and adequately funded should be a given. Achieving it will be complex, but no more so than the digital landscape children themselves learn to navigate. Instead of falling back on a hopeful belief that short-term widely dispersed production funds will find an audience, the need is for a more strategic social intervention. Children's media should be a fundamental part of a review of how we wish to fund public service content.

Above all, though, the need is for a public service children's content provider of scale, with the resources, infrastructure and horizon to mesh with our other national public service providers, including cross-funding. Zammo illustrated how a good storyteller can achieve far more than any government nudge unit. And, incidentally, how it can resonate down the years. Following the release of the Zammo storyline on DVD, the front page of the Daily Star on 9th October 2019 had the headline: BRING BACK GRANGE HILL TO SAVE BRITAIN! How's that for a piece of real-world data?

Hyperbolic and flattering, but I often find myself in conversations with 40–50-somethings, from all walks of life, going out of their way first to ask if something like 'Grange Hill' would work today, then secondly to tell me they wished there was something of its ilk around now. For their own children. To offer a touchstone during the rites of passage journey. Not all the answers but, like that Zammo storyline, pointing to where they might find them. Or at least find a way to start a conversation. Give them strength to contact a helpline.

Finally, another thing British revolutionaries like is the 'least worst' system of everything. So, having been successful once, tried other things and found them wanting, perhaps we should go back to something imperfect but at least better funded. We could, of course, simply bumble along, waiting for the next revolution, or force closure on the current debate. Making the Young Audiences Content Fund a permanent intervention would be a good opener. ⊙

EDUCATION AND THE ROLE OF PUBLIC SERVICE MEDIA

JOHN RICHMOND

During the pandemic we have come to realise the importance of public service media for education. But how did we lose so much of our schools programming and can we get it back?

When I joined Channel 4 in 1992 as Deputy Commissioning Editor, Schools, it had recently taken over responsibility for schools broadcasting from ITV. My colleague and friend Paul Ashton was Commissioning Editor. Over the next eleven years we commissioned television programmes for schools, to be used in classrooms under the guidance of teachers. We commissioned about 35 companies a year, from across the UK, to make the programmes. These companies ranged from the large – some of the ITV companies which had previously formed ITV Schools – to small independents employing a handful of people. In the case of the ITV companies, we commissioned continuations of several series which ITV had for many years produced and broadcast, and which had large and loyal followings amongst teachers and children.

The Broadcasting Act 1990, which among many other measures had imposed on Channel 4 the responsibility for schools broadcasting, required us to broadcast at least 330 hours of schools programmes a year during the school terms. We did our best to ensure that our output was relevant to the school curricula in the four parts of the UK. We had a team of education officers to help us do this. We had a budget of about £10 million a year.

None of this would have happened without public-service regulation. In fact, the very reason for our existence was that government intervention, which had reduced ITV's public-service obligations, had meant that ITV was quite willing to divest itself of a commercial 'burden' which it had honourably carried since schools television began in the UK in the mid-1950s.

All this time, BBC Schools was running an operation about twice our size, paid for by the licence fee. Schools broadcasting in the UK was envied by providers across the world. This achievement had much to do with the talent and commitment of the people who made the programmes. But behind it lay a framework of legislation which enabled that talent and commitment to do its work.

UK children's media, then and now

Beyond education, over many decades, children's media has thrived in the UK. The scale of public-service commitment to children's programmes has been huge. The BBC, ITV, Channel 4, Channel 5 and S4C have distinguished track records, in the first two cases going back many decades to the early days of television. The BBC's and ITV's back catalogues positively heave with titles, across all genres, which adults of several generations recall with pleasure. Today, we contemplate the diversified, fragmenting media environment of the present and the future from a basis of decades of the provision of public-service content for children by the established broadcasters.

This is not to undervalue, culturally or – in a general sense – educatively, the children's content provided more recently by purely commercial channels. Indeed, there are examples of long-running popular series transferring from an established broadcaster to a more recently arrived commercial channel. But no investigation, quantitative or qualitative, will fail to demonstrate the scale, range and diversity of children's content provided by the public-service broadcasters in their heyday.

What do we see as we contemplate the state of public-service media provision for children and young people in the UK in 2021? Put briefly, we see a significant withering-away of provision, except at the BBC.

To begin with the area closest to my own experience: there is no longer anything that could remotely be described as a schools service at Channel 4. The channel's licence from Ofcom, as it stood in 2004, continued to require that the channel should include in its service *"at least 330 hours of schools programmes in each calendar year in the Licensing Period ... to be broadcast in term time or within normal school hours (as Ofcom may agree)."*

The programmes were required to be:

"Of high quality and [...] suitable to meet the needs of schools throughout the United Kingdom.'

The requirement is confirmed in the Annex to the licence:

"The Corporation shall transmit at least 330 hours of schools programmes in each calendar year of the Licensing Period, excluding presentation material. These schools programmes will fulfil the needs of the curriculum and will be supported by a full range of appropriate material."

(Channel 4 Licence, Part 2, paragraph 10(1b) and (2); Annex, Part 1, paragraph 4: December 2004)

In the most recent (2020) version of the channel's licence, the requirement, pursuant to Section 296 of the Communications Act 2003, is that:

"The Corporation shall [...] ensure that the time allocated to Schools Programmes included in the Channel 4 Service constitutes no less than the total amount of time specified in paragraph 4 of Part 1 of the Annex [...] The Corporation shall ensure that any Schools Programmes included in the Channel 4 Service are of high quality and are suitable to meet the needs of schools throughout the United Kingdom."

So, we go to the Annex and we find:

"The Corporation shall transmit at least half an hour of Schools Programmes, excluding presentation material, in each calendar year of the Licensing Period. These Programmes need not be broadcast in term time or within normal school hours."

(Channel 4 Licence, attachment to variation number 20, Part 2, paragraph 10(1b) and (2); and Annex, Part 1, paragraph 4: December 2020)

This is shameful. The suggestion that "at least half an hour of School Programmes" a year (which "need not be broadcast in term time or within normal school hours") will be "suitable to meet the needs of schools throughout the United Kingdom" is extraordinary. It would have been more honest to cancel the service openly. Clearly, the channel's management and the regulator came to some kind of agreement to abandon the service, in fact, while leaving the scantiest of fig leaves in regulation for the look of the thing.

The BBC continues to produce programmes for schools.

Similarly, beyond education, although children's programmes are still to be found on the commercial public-service broadcasters – and I offer no criticisms of their quality – the overall offer from these organisations taken together, in terms of scale, range and diversity, has shrunk dramatically.

BBC Children's continues.

It is not a healthy state of affairs that public-service media for children should overwhelmingly be provided by one source. Ironically, my main argument in support of this assertion is to do with competition: not commercial competition, but competition in quality, in imagination, in innovation. There is no doubt that such competition keeps participants creatively on their toes. (Paul Ashton and I were very much on our toes creatively in the friendly rivalry which existed between BBC Schools and Channel 4 Schools when Channel 4 had a schools service.) And my conversations more widely with children's producers and commissioning executives in all the public-service broadcasters confirm that assertion.

The limitations of the market

However dramatically the media environment has changed in the nearly 30 years since I joined the world of television, the market alone will not, cannot, properly supply all children's needs for education, information and entertainment as supplied by electronic media. My experience in the specialised area of schools media makes that obvious to me. The same is true of children's media more widely. I recognise and welcome many commercial providers' productions for children. In the UK and elsewhere, however, some kinds of programming, in particular indigenous live-action dramas and information programmes for children, as well as educational programmes, are not sufficiently attractive to commercial organisations' balance sheets to make them worth producing. Yet no one – not the commercial organisations themselves – denies the cultural and experiential value to children of having access to a broad range and rich diversity of media experiences. Such experiences are an investment in the future.

An example of 'investment in the future'

This example is current. As I write, schools across the UK have just re-opened after long periods during which they were closed to all but children of critical workers and those who are vulnerable for other reasons. The emergency visited on the world by Covid-19 has had an enormous impact on all sections of society, in the UK and across the world, but all the evidence is that socio-economically poorer families have been hit the hardest, and that the children of those families will suffer the worst as a result of the interruption to their education. This is because they are less likely to have sophisticated equipment to receive educational media in their homes, and less likely to have the quiet spaces conducive to concentrated study. This has been true for many years: Livingstone et al. (2005) conclude that "middle class children are more likely to have access to the internet at home and to use it. With regard to the current situation, a recent medical study notes that "for some children the lack of internet, electronic devices, and quiet space at home will further exacerbate inequalities in educational outcomes" (Sinha et al., 2020). All generalisations of this kind are dangerous if applied glibly, but there is truth in them nonetheless.

In these circumstances, what commercial organisation rapidly stepped up to provide educational media, virtually free at the point of use, to – at worst – mitigate the damage done by the closure of schools and – at best – give the pleasure and fulfilment which successful learning affords, even if it does take place in a cramped bedroom or on the corner of a dining table? The BBC, at short notice, supplied a rich variety of educational media to support home learning. Now, it may be that it could have done even better than it did, as the UK's premier public-service media provider, to meet the emergency. But the key point is that in this crisis a non-market player, a public-service entity, at least did something, and something significant, to rise to the challenge. And why was the BBC in a position to move as quickly as it did? Because it has an enviably large library of content, accumulated over many years, paid for by the licence fee.

My numerous contacts over the last year with schoolteachers, school governors and the parents of school-age children have offered me frequent testimony to the value which they have put on the BBC's recent support for home learning. A school governor of a rural primary school in England, who has special responsibility for the safeguarding of children who may be at risk, has told me that she is sure that the service has been a lifeline in some households where the adults are not confident or competent in undertaking even a modest amount of home education for their children.

In sum...

To summarise my argument so far:
- I welcome the diverse range of providers of content intended to educate, inform and entertain children in the UK;
- I have no animus whatever against commercial providers offering such content;
- however, as things stand, commercial providers, by the nature of their obligations to shareholders, will not willingly invest in content which is unlikely to pay its way;
- therefore, however excellent much of the commercially provided content may be, there are serious gaps in overall provision;

- only a non-commercial funding model will guarantee the range and diversity of genres of and contexts for children's content which children have a right to expect;

- I recognise that the maintenance of a place for public-service media for children has become a more complex matter to legislate for and organise, given the proliferation of channels, means of carriage and receiving devices;

- so, we need to find a model which can live and thrive in this proliferated environment, while continuing to offer to future generations of children the experience which, at its best, the various public-service broadcasters of the past and present – the BBC, ITV, Channel 4, Channel 5 and S4C – have offered to yesterday's children;

- it is regrettable that the public-service responsibility for children's media, including educational media, has largely – not entirely, I admit – devolved onto one organisation.

What do we do about this?

In order to answer the question effectively, I need briefly to venture beyond the limits of the title of this essay, and to make a proposal about the funding of public-service media generally.

Paying for public-service media

I believe that the licence fee, raised as a quasi-tax and given in its entirety to the BBC, is reaching the end of its useful life as a way of paying for public-service media. Equally, I vigorously reject the arguments of those who would turn the BBC loose into the commercial world, probably as a subscription service, with customers choosing whether or not to buy into it at various levels of cost. Often, the ideological nature of these attacks on the current method of funding the BBC is disguised by appeals to technological modernity: "In the age of Netflix, how can something as antiquated at the licence fee be justified?" Behind such arguments stand powerful media and political interests which would like to see the wholesale privatisation of UK broadcasting, as in the USA (where the only exception is PBS, which relies for its continuing existence on the generosity of individuals and wealthy organisations), and the abandonment of UK broadcasters' obligation to be impartial politically. The equivalents of Fox News and MSNBC would be born in the UK.

I accept that there are also less ideological voices who would keep the obligation on UK broadcasters to be impartial, but who still think that the licence fee should be scrapped and replaced by a subscription system. If this happened, the BBC's ability to appeal to and serve the whole community in the UK would immediately be savagely reduced, as would its ability to project 'soft power' across a world increasingly in the control of autocrats with no interest in factually accurate reporting. Additionally, the BBC has an important responsibility to keep the whole nation informed in cases of national emergency; and it has been doing precisely that as the Covid-19 pandemic has continued. This responsibility could not be fulfilled under a subscription system, except by some awkward ad-hoc arrangement whereby the Government would give the BBC temporary funds to keep the whole population informed when it deemed that a national emergency was at hand.

But the licence fee is imperfect, and its principal imperfection is that it's regressive: the Duke of Westminster pays the same amount to access BBC services as does someone on the minimum wage. The argument against funding the BBC from direct taxation is the old one about the corporation not being a state broadcaster: it should have the right to challenge and criticise the Government without risking its funds being cut off. But the licence fee is effectively a tax, imposed after a conversation between the Government and the BBC every 15 years. I don't see that a hypothecated tax, raised by other means, needs to compromise the BBC's independence from Government. It could be imposed either as a specified addition to Income Tax or to Council Tax. In either case, there is a degree of progressivism: obvious in the case of an addition to Income Tax; less obvious but still there in the case of an addition to Council Tax, which is banded according to the rateable value of property.

So, my proposal for a replacement of the licence fee would be a hypothecated tax, attached either to income tax or to Council Tax.

Public-service funding for children's media spread across the board

I would set the rate of the tax so that it raises a little more money – between 5% and 10% more – than the licence fee does at the moment. The great majority of these funds – at least 90% – would go to the BBC, ensuring that it continues to be funded to at least its present level. But an amount beyond the BBC's share would go to other media providers, whether those who retain public-service status (ITV, Channel 4, Channel 5 and S4C) or straightforwardly commercial organisations, for the commissioning of public-service content in a group of specified areas, including children's media other than media for schools.

Why "other than media for schools", given my earlier remarks about the abandonment of the Channel 4 schools service? Simply because that lamentable situation can easily be rectified: Ofcom should once again require Channel 4 to have a high-quality schools service at meaningful scale. Demand for educational programming has been demonstrated in the past: in the loyalty conversion rates for Teachers TV (McMahon, 2008) and in teacher accounts of its value (Tanner, 2006); while evidence for demand for the continuation of TV provision by the BBC and Channel 4 in the face of alternative online provision is well documented in the longer history of programming for schools (e.g. Moss, 2000; Chien, 1999). Ofcom's extensive consultation on the state and future of public-service media shows that today's audiences value its distinctive content highly, including educational provison (Ofcom, 2020). Current demand has increased due to the coronavirus pandemic, leading – as I have described above – to the BBC's rapid expansion in provision of both online and broadcast resources, with a marked shift to television to offset limited access to broadband and devices (BBC, 2021), a trend against the longer-term decline in general broadcast viewing (Ofcom, 2019).

With regard to children's media other than provision for schools, an expert commissioning group, taking account of the BBC's offer in this area, would agree where overall provision was lacking or where creative competition would enhance that provision, would invite bids from organisations other than the BBC to produce content to meet those needs, and would oversee production. With the help of a non-executive board, it would judge the quality and the take-up of the content so provided. 'Take-up' of course means reception across the full range of platforms and receiving devices to which children and young people have access.

Fortunately, such an expert commissioning group already exists. The Young Audiences Content Fund, based at the British Film Institute, is currently funding a wide range of content and development in children's media. It has a budget of £57 million for a three-year pilot, funded by some unused licence fee money originally earmarked for a digital project at the BBC. It is headed by a former executive at BBC Children's. To quote from its website, the YACF:

"Supports the creation of distinctive, high-quality content for audiences up to the age of 18 [...] Production and development awards will contribute to the funding of programmes, shown on television and online platforms, that have public-service broadcasting values in live-action and animation and across all genres. We are looking for content that entertains, informs and reflects the experiences of children and young people growing up in the UK today."

These ambitions and this expertise are exactly what we need longer term. The YACF, its personnel expanded if necessary, funded by its share of the hypothecated tax, could be charged with seeing that public-service media for children and young people in the UK, supplied by numerous providers alongside the BBC, has a thriving future.

In conclusion

I conclude with the thought that when the UK sported two and then three, four and five public-service broadcasters, in a technologically relatively simple world, those broadcasters' offer to children and young people in the areas of education, information and entertainment was the envy of much of the rest of the world. There is no reason, in today's and tomorrow's technologically relatively complex world, why that excellence should not be maintained, if the right policy decisions are taken. Those who serve children's and young people's media needs and choices retain both the necessary talent and the underlying passion for the task.

References

BBC News (2021) 'Lockdown Learning: What educational resources are on TV, iPlayer and online?' Accessed 11.3.21 at https://www.bbc.co.uk/news/education-55591821

Chien, M-Y. (1999) 'The Contribution of the Characteristics of Schools Programmes to their Use in English Primary Schools'. Journal of Educational Media, Volume 24(3).

Livingstone, S., Bober, M. and Helsper, E. (2005) 'Inequalities and the digital divide in children and young people's internet use: findings from the UK Children Go Online project'. London: London School of Economics and Political Science.

McMahon, A. (2008) 'Teachers TV: Education Analysis Report'. London: DCMS.

Moss, R. (2000) 'Closing a window on the world: Convergence and UK television services for schools'. Cultural Trends, Volume 10(40).

Ofcom (2019) 'Children and parents: Media use and attitudes report 2019'. London: Ofcom.

Ofcom (2020) 'Small Screen: Big Debate – Consultation: The Future of Public Service Media'. London: Ofcom.

Sinha, I., Bennett, D. and Taylor-Robinson, D. (2020) 'Children are being side-lined by Covid-19'. theBMJ (369). Accessed 12.3.21 at https://www.bmj.com/content/369/bmj.m2061

Tanner, R. (2006) 'Unexpected Outcomes from Teachers' TV'. Mathematics Teaching Incorporating Micromath, number 199, pp. 28-30.

Acknowledgements

I thank Andrew Burn and Anna Home for significant improvements and additions to this essay.

PUBLIC SERVICE BROADCASTING FOR CHILDREN AND THE COMMERCIAL PSBS

EMERITA PROFESSOR MÁIRE MESSENGER DAVIES

An eminent children's media professor gives her perspective on the context for this debate and the importance of understanding how children's media experiences are changing and the extent to which there is continuity.

As I write, it is World Book Day and my social media timelines are full of children dressed as the Gruffalo, and Paddington, and the Worst Witch, all characters from books that they have both read and, more likely, seen on television. The relationship between children's books and TV shows is symbiotic and has been from television's beginning, as Anna Home, former head of children's BBC, describes in her book about British children's television, *Into the Box of Delights* (1993)[1] – the 'Box of Delights' being itself the title of a book by John Masefield, dramatized for children by the BBC in 1984.

However, although children's book publishing – a highly commercial enterprise – receives the kind of culturally respectable attention conferred by a special day, the same never happens for children's television. Why should this be? This article takes a look at some of the value and other judgements lying behind the never-ending effort – the 'fight' to use Home's word - to get children's television the appreciation it deserves, the most recent bout being this very campaign by the Children's Media Foundation (CMF).

It is all the more galling that these special-attention events never happen for children's television, because sometimes the TV version is better than the book, in my opinion. As Anna Home reminded me in a recent interview,[2] looking back on her own long career in children's television, "Children's has never been considered top class stuff [within the industry]. It's always been a fight for recognition, for money." And yet a lot of it *is* 'top class stuff'. I loved the *Demon Headmaster* books by Gillian Cross but I thought the 1990s TV versions were more scientifically complex, dramatic and thought-provoking, and they were a huge hit with the audience, beating even adult shows in the ratings. It was good to discover – thanks to my nine-year-old granddaughter – that there is a new version of '*The Demon Headmaster*' (CBBC, 2019). But I would not have discovered it from any fanfares on the part of adult show-business media or even from the Radio Times, which once had regular special pages devoted to children. And when it comes to more 'top class stuff', look no further than '*Horrible Histories*', still going strong on CBBC. Terry Deary's books are great. But when you add the songs, the costumes and the brilliant comic actors and scriptwriters, you have a television masterpiece. In 2011, HH won Best Sketch Show at the British Comedy Awards – a remarkable achievement for a 'mere' children's programme.

Note that all these shows I've mentioned are from the BBC. The BBC is described by Patrick Barwise and Peter York in their recent book, '*The War against the BBC*'[3], as the main source of children's public service material currently, and so it is. But it was not always so. When we conducted our study about children's television published in 'Dear BBC',[4] with over 1400 children around the UK, ITV programmes competed on an equal footing with BBC. In one of the sample weeks that we studied, '*Byker Grove*', the BBC's children's 'soap' set in the North East, and '*Blue Peter*', competed with ITV's comedy '*Woof!*', and the informative '*How2*' (thankfully now resurrected in a new series, '*How*', on CITV). In the children's top tens, ITV's dramas '*The Tomorrow People*' and '*Children's Ward*' competed on equal terms with the BBC's '*Byker Grove*', and '*Grange Hill*'.

Children's broadcasting and regulation

Nowadays, there is a much less substantial thread of PSB provision on the commercial channels – CITV, C4 and C5. The fact that there is any at all is no thanks to legislation. In the 1990 Broadcasting Act, children's programming was made a protected category, partly thanks to a campaign from producers, researchers, parents and activists, in a group which was a precursor of CMF, called British Action for Children's Television (BACTV). Commercial PSBs – ITV, Channel 4, Channel 5 – were awarded licenses on condition that they provided generically diverse material, accessible to different age groups, at times when children were available to view. The 2003 Broadcasting Act dropped this requirement, and, allied to the 'junk food' advertising ban of 2006, led to the commercial PSBs ceasing to provide children's programming on the same scale as they had done previously. According to the 2003 law, children were no longer seen as an audience that a public service broadcaster was bound to serve. Imagine if there'd been a similar law defunding children's libraries.

The latest regulations regarding children, as expressed in the channels' various broadcasting codes (see websites)[5] say nothing about providing diverse, age-appropriate content as the 1990 Act provisions did. The only regulations relating to children concern the protection of child performers – a very important consideration of course (see Davies and Mosdell, 2001).[6] Nevertheless, there is still some content provision on the commercial PSBs, not least because it is clearly in broadcasters' own interest to cultivate young audiences, as Alan Horrox, formerly of Thames TV and Tetra Productions, pointed out to us in our 'Dear BBC' study:

"Broadcasters need children because they grow up into adult audiences, which is what broadcasters need [...] The second commercial reason is [...] there's a very, very sizeable adult market for children's products which children are crucially influential in. It's also a fundamental fact for all channels to feel young, including middle-aged audiences like myself, youth is a tremendous asset."[7]

ITV's CITV is an all-day channel, consisting mainly of animations, many of them American, and some repeated from previous years. One interesting feature that positively distinguishes it from the better-resourced CBBC is that it runs all day from 6.00 and on into prime time, ceasing at 9.00. Some of the material in this later, very competitive slot, is aimed at older children, and I caught an extraordinary drama series called 'World of Weird', about an Australian family with rather disturbing zombie parents, living in an Irish B & B, a house that looked as if it had once belonged to Father Ted – a comedy echo supported by its casting of Pauline McGlynn as the local school's head teacher. The final CITV show at 8.30 pm was a sparky documentary, 'Mission Employable', a really innovative programme using young presenters, doing signing and voiceover to explain to children, both hearing impaired and not, how to get a job as a gardener, with gardening tips added. I loved this, and I do hope that its intended audience has been finding it. Channel 5 has a three-hour dedicated slot for young children early every morning – Milkshake!. Most of the shows are animation but 'The World According to Grandpa', is an innovatory exception; it is mainly live action, with the magisterial Don Warrington, of 'Death in Paradise' and much other fame, explaining electricity to his little granddaughter, first via a charming folk tale, then with the real science. This show is one of the programmes helped by funding from the Young Audiences Content Fund (YACF), a £60 million grant from the DCMS, administered by the BFI, to support children's production – some of the programmes it has supported are listed below. It goes without saying that the commercial channels' programmes are interspersed with a great deal of advertising, mainly of toys. Channel 4, once a bastion of educational programming, is not providing any children's material at the moment that I could see but, again, thanks to the YACF, it produced a one-off special at Christmas 2020, Quentin Blake's 'Clown'.

The importance of 'place'

One-off specials aren't enough, though. If we're thinking of true public service value, we have to bear in mind the unique characteristics of the child audience, especially young children, and the fact that their lives are constrained by other schedules. Favourite activities need to be predictable. All the digital channels do recognise this. Their slots and regular programmes are in the same place and time (though way down on the EPG), and children (and, perhaps more importantly, parents) know where to find them every day. And the programmes, though recorded, exist in a 'real-world' situation; they are topped and tailed with actual presenters talking to the actual audience, featuring actual children in the audience and their actual birthdays and pets. The value of this direct address – an important public service value – is that it signals this territory belongs to them. The idea of a children's schedule as protected space goes right back to the beginning of children's television, as Home's book describes. Despite the media's uncoupling of the real world from the digital one, and the irrelevance of real time and place made possible by technology, children's lives do still depend on regular daily scheduling and a sense that they are part of the public sphere as things happen. Children also still rely on having kind, dependable adults to talk directly to them, and all the children's channels' presenters fulfil this function.

However, there is one area for older children which – as also for adults – absolutely must be rooted in the here-and-now, and that is news. The commercial PSBs do not provide children's news programmes as they once did (for example, Channel 4's '*First Edition*') although, aided by the Young Audiences Content Fund, Sky Kids offers a weekly news programme called '*FYI News specials*', which deal with issues of particular relevance to children and "explainers to help children to understand events in the news and in their lives." But the BBC has offered children's news continuously since '*Newsround*' was introduced in 1972; and, given the BBC's privileged position and funding as the primary public service broadcaster in the UK, so it should.

At the beginning of the pandemic last year, when children could no longer go to school and had to learn at home, the BBC earned praise for the way it immediately cleared BBC2's schedules to air Bitesize educational and informational programmes for children – a true public service response. Almost simultaneously, the regulator Ofcom allowed the BBC to cut back its provision of the award-winning '*Newsround*' from 85 to 35 hours a year and to reduce broadcast bulletins on children's channel CBBC from three to one a day in favour of on-demand distribution on the CBBC/Newsround website and on iPlayer. This was despite objections from a variety of groups, such as producers, the Children's Media Foundation, the Voice of the Listener and Viewer, educators and academic researchers. If ever there was a case of bad timing, it was this. Once the scale of the Covid-19 crisis was known, and children (and parents) had been forced out of their everyday routines to face a frightening and very uncertain future, it would have been a true act of public service to put '*Newsround*' back where it was before 2013 – at 5.00 on BBC1.

I realise this is an extremely radical suggestion, but why not be radical in times like these? Putting Bitesize on BBC2 was radical; hiring 'celebrity supply teachers' like Marcus Rashford, for the CBBC schedule was radical, too. Imagine if '*Newsround*' had been aired just after the regular press conferences from Downing Street, with an explanation of what the announcements meant for children and their families. Imagine if some '*Newsround*' reporters, including the programme's young reporters, could have asked some questions on behalf of the nation's children and young people. Instead, this radical show (still doing a good informative, if much curtailed job) can only be caught live early in the morning, repeated in the evening. There is, of course, news material on its website, but there is still evidence that children prefer news in live broadcast form rather than searching the web for it (see also Carter et al, 2009).[8]

Where is the child audience?

But do children watch TV anymore? Aren't they surfing the web all the time and watching other people playing games on YouTube? I was struck, when looking at Ofcom's latest (2019)[9] data for children's viewing habits, by the fact that the majority of 5-15 year olds (74%) watch programmes as live (i.e., when broadcast), compared with 61% for SVoD (e.g., Netflix) and 49% on catchup. What surprised me even more was that the figures for 3-4 year olds and 12-15 year olds watching TV 'live', were exactly the same – 75%. When it comes to VoD, as we might expect, the older children increasingly outnumber younger ones until we get 88% versus 65% in these two age groups. The Ofcom data also show that these high numbers of children watching material, as aired, have hardly changed in the last five years. The child audience these days is sometimes seen as hard to find, compared to the 1990s and early 2000s, because of all the new platforms and because of the internet; much academic research on children now focuses on their use of online digital material. The TV set which we have all learned to love again during the pandemic (see The Guardian, Saturday February 6, 2021), seems currently to be of less scholarly interest. I would suggest that this lack of attention to the importance of broadcast TV is a mistake. And it would seem that the BBC agrees with me; it has recently announced that the digital-only BBC3, having produced many programmes popular with the ever-elusive youth audience, is returning as a broadcast channel.

Hope for the future

This seems to me a promising development. The Young Audiences' Content Fund[10] mentioned above, the £60 million grant from the DCMS, administered by the BFI, to support the production of children's content across channels other than the BBC, is another hopeful development. Some examples of programmes supported by the fund are:

- *'Sali Mali'* - S4C - (ages 0 to 4) – in Welsh
- *'Go Green With The Grimwades'* - Channel 5 - (ages 0 to 7) – environmental issues / protecting the environment
- *'The World According To Grandpa'* - Channel 5 & S4C (ages 0 to 7) – cross generational family dynamics
- Quentin Blake's *'Clown'* Channel 4 (ages 0 to 11)
- *'Lacklan, Boy at the Top'* - BBC ALBA - (ages 8 to 11) – Scottish Gaelic
- *'Rùn'* BBC ALBA - ages (8 to 11) - Scottish Gaelic
- *'Sol'* - BBC ALBA- (ages 8 to 11) – teaching elements of grief – created in Celtic languages Irish, Welsh and Scottish Gaelic
- *'Don't Unleash the Beast'* CITV (ages 8 to 11)
- *'How'* – CITV - (ages 8 to 11)
- *'FYI News Specials Sky'* – (ages 12 to 14)
- *'Letters on Lockdown'* - E4/All4 – (ages 12 to 18)
- *'Rap Therapy'* Channel 4 - (ages 12 to 18) – teaching kids about mental health
- *'First Dates: Teens'* - E4 - (ages 16-24)[11]

The current funding project is a three-year pilot, but judging from the diverse and imaginative collection of programmes in the above list, it is to be hoped that it gets put on a more permanent footing.

Why does children's programming matter?

When it comes to answering this question, Anna Home continues to make the point first made in an interview in 1997:

"Children have a culture which is very specific, and although they watch programming that isn't made for them, they need programming which is geared to their own culture, and their own perception and their own levels of awareness, and just as I don't think anyone should say let's kill off children's literature, I don't think anyone should say let's kill off children's television."[12]

Not only should they not kill it off, they should celebrate it. Maybe we should think about a World Children's TV Day?

References

[1] Home, A. (1993) 'Into the Box of Delights: A history of children's television'. London: BBC Books

[2] Anna Home interview with M. M. Davies, February 2nd, 2021

[3] Barwise, P. and York, P. (2020) 'The War against the BBC: How an unprecedented combination of hostile forces is destroying Britain's greatest cultural institution . . . And why you should care'. Dublin: Penguin/Random House

[4] Messenger Davies, M. (2001) 'Dear BBC: Children, television storytelling and the public sphere', Cambridge: CUP.

[5] Broadcasting Codes

https://www.itv.com/commissioning/articles/compliance-guidelines

https://www.bbc.co.uk/editorialguidelines/guidelines

https://www.channel4.com/producers-handbook/

https://static.skyassets.com/contentstack/assets/bltdc2476c7b6b194dd/blte199b9f7f7aa0e5e/5d9b46e973942313e3c431a3/Editorial_Compliance_Pack_Oct_2019.pdf

[6] Messenger Davies, M. and Mosdell, N. (2001) 'Consenting children? The use of children in non-fiction television programmes', London: Broadcasting Standards Commission

[7] Interviewed in Messenger Davies, M. (2001) 'Dear BBC', ibid.

[8] Carter, C., Messenger Davies, M., Allan, S., Mendes, K., Prince, I. and Wass, L. 2009. 'What do children want from the BBC?' Available at https://www.bbc.co.uk/blogs/knowledgeexchange/cardifftwo.pdf.

[9] 'Children's media use and attitudes' report, 2019. London: Ofcom

[10] YACFund website https://www2.bfi.org.uk/supporting-uk-film/production-development-funding/young-audiences-content-fund

[11] Thanks to Charlotte Prentice, of Multitude Media North, for this information.

[12] 'Dear BBC' ibid. and Anna Home interview with M. M. Davies, February 2nd, 2021

UNDERSTANDING THE MEDIA EXPERIENCES OF TODAY'S CHILDREN

Photo by Bruce Mars on Unsplash

THE PHYSICAL AND THE VIRTUAL: UNDERSTANDING CHILDREN'S RELATIONSHIPS WITH THEIR MEDIA

ANNE LONGFIELD

A former Children's Commissioner draws on a lifetime of working with children to explore the way their media experiences are changing out of all recognition.

I'm not a public service media expert but I do know about kids. And right from the beginning of my six years as Children's Commissioner, the digital world was something I looked at in depth, seeing it in the context of the whole of a child's life.

Previous generations thought of the digital world as some kind of add on: remember the early days when you had to unplug a phone and put a cable into the wall? How long ago was that? 25 years? If you go back ten years, it became a bit more sophisticated, but there was still a sense of the digital world as something that you chose to engage with for a certain period of time and then you went back to your real life. Whereas for kids that have grown up in the last ten years, that separation is just nowhere in their perceptions. Now, even I see the digital world and the physical world as virtually merged into one, and certainly kids will always say they see it as the same thing.

All they have known is an existence where there is a physical and a digital community or a series of digital communities, screens and environments that have the ability to merge. And it is the kids themselves who are curating this. Perhaps in quite a clunky way sometimes, but they're the ones doing it: creating their own portfolios, their own collections of stuff that they like and want to watch or to be part of their world. They have to go to different places to bring it together but they're doing it.

The next stage in this merging of digital communities would be to consider how that process can be refined and, indeed, should it be refined? Perhaps we should be asking is it a good thing? But it seems that refining it is inevitable because children are doing it now.

In considering this next stage, is there a role for public service media or a regulator to offer leadership? Who will look after the community or make sure that community is safe? What mechanisms need to be in place to ensure kids aren't just left to spend their time in environments that no one knows about or without an element of safety or responsibility in there?

The moment smart phones became affordable, that's the moment everything changed for kids. Now they have one entry point for a whole range of viewing platforms. But where does public service media sit in that? It seems to me that, for kids, the traditional broadcast companies aren't yet an integral part of their experience. I've been shocked by how many children have told me that they view very little in real time and they don't watch mainstream TV channels. They don't even think about them. They don't know what the BBC is, and I think that will be a huge shock to a lot of adults. We know that younger adults have wider viewing habits, but it is children too. They say to me, "We don't watch BBC." Then they'll say, "Yes, we know what it is but there is nothing there for us."

If public service media is supposed to serve the public, it is worth remembering that children are 20% of the population. Right now, children have to make the choice to go to public service media rather than public service media making the choice to go to the children's audience. Children need to find their lives reflected in what they view. Their needs need to be served. They have a right to get a look in but, at the moment, they don't believe that is happening. They feel underserved.

I think about the shows that shaped my life or my kids' lives. I have a pet theory, untested, about 'Neighbours' and the impact it had on kids' culture. I was working directly with kids at that point, and they all wanted to watch the show after school. My observations, when this show was at its most popular, were that this was the moment when kids first thought it normal to talk about their feelings. 'Neighbours' was touchy-feely in that way, and there was something about the language around feelings and emotions that became much more mainstream with kids. I have no idea if that theory plays out in any scientific analysis, but the show was a massive part of children's media experiences at that time. Sure, it's not public service media, or even aimed at children, but it makes the point about the huge impact media experiences can have on children's development.

The question now is if children aren't watching real-time TV, where are they getting those influences in terms of their media experiences? And are they influences that are positive? Do they have a collective reference point or are they individualistic because each child is having to find their own? Are they being short-changed by that or is it actually a positive thing that we need to embrace and find a way to support?

Kids talk about influencers not in terms of a particular place or platform, but as characters in their lives. They don't segment in the same way that adults do. It's either about what they like or what their friends are watching, and they will have their own catalogue of things they go to: some things will be very simple, like watching people drawing unicorns, or perhaps watching people watching things. I found 6–11-year-olds are really into how you make stuff. So these people become their influencers, and this leaves adults with few reference points as to where their children are going or what they are doing.

It seems like a strange new world in its own right and not an add-on to our real, physical world.

And public service media is having to play catch up. Yes, it was so much easier when there were just a few channels, but for children now, that idea is abhorrent. "How could you even exist? Were dinosaurs around at the time?" We need to find mechanisms that help individuals to find meaningful ways to live in this new world, which children are currently navigating by themselves.

So, how can public service media help? Kids really benefit from the validation they get from seeing themselves in stories. In fiction they are able to explore and get the validation of their view of the world and also see that it isn't just about them. Children that are maybe a bit quirky, or feel they're the odd one out or shy, or have a particular challenge in their life; there's something reassuring in having that experience reflected to them through fiction. And I do think there is a role for public service media. Just as we've had a renaissance in books over the last year in many ways, there is something here about programmes and fiction on screen: there's a potential there to help, we just have to find it.

Playing out scenarios is how children come to terms with things and are able to share their worries. For example, putting masks on their dolls during the pandemic. Children's programmes in the past have done this brilliantly, dealing with issues like relationships or drugs. There is still a need for this sort of content. At the moment, there is a lot of discussion around relationships, sexual assault in school and societal attitudes towards women and girls. What is consent? What is a relationship? What is banter? There's a real role there for public service media and clearly a need for those issues to be explored, but to do it in a clever way is the prize.

And of course it needs to be joined up across platforms but also linked in with schools as well. I doubt there is a secondary school in the land that doesn't have some kind of review going on in terms of their response to, at least, reports of sexual assault. I think there is a role for schools to proactively look at how they can support a much more positive understanding of the impact of an individual's actions and be a positive force for change.

The BBC already has a very strong relationship with schools, so there is an opening there for something that could go to the next level in terms of agility across different problems. To tackle these issues in a way that isn't clunky but fun and meaningful and engaging. Those are the great strengths of drama. Can you imagine how grateful parents would be if a public service media provider could pull that off? But kids need to be able to find that content. Public service content-makers need to understand how kids piece things together and utilise that.

Setting aside the online safety element, right now, I see danger in two ways and both to do with the volume of content. Kids tell me they worry that the range of content that comes to them is getting narrower and narrower. The algorithms figure out what they like and take them to more of the same. My worry is that their view of the world at a very young age starts to become very narrow. We all do it; I set my news update to never send any sport and I can forget sport even exists, and it's a pleasant place to be for me. But if you are a child and you get a really narrow procurement of news or views or ideas, you don't have the breadth of experience in life to remember there are other things going on.

The other concern is that there's just so much quantity of media, they get swamped by the enormity of the content and end up swimming around in a lot stuff which will be of poor quality, struggling to find stuff they actually like.

So, there is that weird paradox of the two things; either really narrow stuff which is lessening the world view, or just the sheer volume of stuff that keeps coming and kids struggle to find their way through. This seems to demand a better way. Again, maybe there is an opportunity here for public service media to actually take that leadership role and provide some mechanisms for children to be able to curate their world in a more child-appropriate way, but also in a way that gets over those hurdles. That enables children to keep that overview but not have to wade through so much content that it is just mind-numbing.

The last year has been interesting in terms of digital usage. For all of us, our screens have taken on a different meaning and different status in our lives, and whereas parents previously would have worried about children spending too much time on screens, over the last year a lot of the rules that were there before have been relaxed enormously. I guess the question that comes out of the last year is where does that leave us? It's almost been like a live lab test. Where are kids in their various communities? How have they found their way through? They've spent so much time online, are they managing it themselves now because they've had enough? Are they bored with screens because the novelty has gone and seeing a person face to face is much more appealing? Or have they now got so much content that they are lost in it? Do they need to be able to recreate their ability to function in the physical world?

There is an opportunity to see what's happened over this year, but to also reset a little as we go forward: how do we manage this duality of existence?

I really welcome the fact schools are spending more time talking about wellbeing and mental health, and I hope that will continue. But in children's broader lives too, the whole move back into whatever the next stage of normality is for kids will be really crucial. Parents who had been furloughed going back to work, kids back in school, entertainment opening up in places, more people about: there's a danger that some children might, through no fault of their family, have a period where there are big changes going on in their life and adults are too busy to see what that might mean for them. And in that situation, reliance and engagement in a digital environment might not be a positive experience. Absolutely there should be regulation to protect children online, but positive public service media can also play a preventative role here, building children's resilience against harmful experiences in these anxious times.

Children need age-appropriate content, but they could also be celebrated more in mainstream content. We have moved on from 'children should be seen and not heard', but they still aren't celebrated at the heart of our communities in the way some other countries do. If you go to Norway, it's very clear that children are a high priority. It has struck me over the pandemic that in Norway and in several other countries, New Zealand for example, there were public service broadcasts very early on about the pandemic specifically for kids. There were reassuring messages from the prime minister in those countries, and, as Children's Commissioner, I was keen to get something like that here in the UK, but it was just too difficult for people to organise.

There's a job to be done here to raise the profile of children's needs in our public discourse and give more of a role for children's characters and presenters within mainstream programmes, as well as in specialist programmes for children.

You can't compartmentalise children's education from their play, and their media is part of everything. It's all one and the same. Whichever environment they're in, or whichever phase of digital development we're in, children's needs are just the same. And now because they don't see the joins, it's even more important that adults understand the digital world is not just a peripheral part of existence. Kids have had global, multimillion pound companies dominating their life for the last few years. We all have. And it's like everyone has been blinded by the light of what they can do for you: get your shopping fast, speak to your friends ... and it's all amazing. But the balance of power between the users and the suppliers in this case isn't in the right place. The seesaw is way down on the multibillion pound companies that are feeding us this stuff. We need to get a better balance, and I think the acceptance of that is part of a maturing digital world. Platforms and companies need to accept that with this position they have in people's lives comes responsibility. If they lose their users' trust, they lose everything. They'll only keep that trust if they show they're acting responsibility.

And, of course, trust is something that the traditional public service broadcasters have had, but now they are playing catch up. It is in their self-interest to do more for children. This is their future audience. Yet 80% of that 12-14-year-old audience say they have no experience of the BBC. If you want to engage kids, you have to go where they are, and on their terms, rather than trying to get them to fit into your way of doing things. You cannot force them into an adult infrastructure. To engage with them, engage how they engage. Go where they are and fit in with their lives. And ask children and co-create with them.

That can't just be about meeting the needs of children today, because their world is changing so much that, actually, it needs to be a constant collaboration with them. Maybe part of that mechanism is how can they be active participants, shaping what they actually view in a more dynamic way. I can imagine that is difficult for public service media, where there is a strong emphasis on responsibility, on control and reassurance. Finding a way that doesn't dilute those values but enables children to have a collaborative and engaged role in their media is an enormous challenge, and I don't have the answer. But I do believe that is what children want, and if the review into the future of public service media is to meet the needs of the children's audience, we need to start thinking what the answer might be. ◔

CARRYING THE BATON: BBC CHILDREN'S & EDUCATION

PATRICIA HIDALGO

The Director of Children's & Education at the BBC makes the case for the provision of public service media at scale through a healthy, high-quality commissioning slate. The article also highlights the value of restoring public service competition for UK children's attention through initiatives like the Young Audience's Content Fund.

Since becoming the Director of BBC Children's and Education last September it has been a real honour and pleasure to become involved in the delivery of public service edutainment for children, this being my motivation for moving across from the commercial TV sector.

Because of our unique publicly funded position it's not for me or the BBC to suggest how the wider market might be shaped in the future, but I hope I can usefully share some of my thoughts as to how I see us continuing to evolve and deliver a top-class public service that entertains, educates and informs young audiences.

The best thing about my time in this role so far has been overseeing content for children that really makes a difference. Back in January we reacted quickly to deliver Lockdown Learning, an initiative to reach all UK children with a mix of educational and edutainment content to help them keep learning during schools' shutdown. It meant rapid-turnaround collaborations across all areas of Children's and Education and with the support of the wider BBC. I was extremely proud to witness the positive reaction of the public and the value it brought families at a difficult national time. This is a great example of what only the BBC can do, and we are going to continue providing this educational and edutainment content beyond the pandemic, making another 30 hours of TV programmes this year – part of an ongoing resource for children and teachers, online and on TV, so we can reach everyone through our BBC Bitesize websites, our CBBC and CBeebies networks and, of course, with BBC iPlayer.

With inclusion and diversity being such an important subject for society right now, I have also taken great pride in the range of content we make that addresses this subject, some of which we recently created to celebrate UK Black History. Not just one piece but many formats for all ages, celebrating our Black History heroes, as well as a 'Horrible Histories British Black History' special for our 7+ audience, or our 'Magic Hands' format for both D/deaf and hearing pre-schoolers celebrating Black History songs on CBeebies, not to forget an extensive range of educational content on BBC Bitesize, including the experiences of soldiers from the Caribbean and South Africa in World War One. Being free from the commercial pressures of advertising and set schedules, we have the ability to respond to current themes our audience is exposed to with bespoke content to inform, educate and enrich their lives, their curiosity and understanding of the world around them.

I've highlighted the output above to underline that we are in the business of delivering public service content for children – it's not a discussion topic for us, it's what we do. And by 'public service' I mean a range of innovative and high-quality content reflecting and representing UK culture and communities, delivered in a safe space that parents and children can easily access. The BBC has always been at the heart of UK public service provision at scale. But we face large challenges.

The biggest one is remaining relevant to kids. We all believe that public service media matters. Our audience needs to believe it too. We have to make content which is both nourishing and that they want to consume. It's imperative that children can see British values, culture, locations and diverse representation in all genres: drama, factual, comedy and, under our latest plans, animation. But being British and public service isn't a reason in itself for kids to choose us. They are used to and enjoy children's content from all around the world that other platforms, including global giants, provide for them, and competition is getting harder and harder.

I'm glad to say that we still reach an enormous audience – across TV and iPlayer, BBC Children's combine for over 1.2bn minutes of content viewing every week. Yet there is huge pressure on our TV channels where, like everyone else, we have seen the impact of the big-tech platforms.

Policymakers and parents have a big stake in what we do, quite rightly. They have a tendency to always evaluate our content from the same angle: that it should be educational. Important, but it misses something vital. Our output mix must be highly entertaining, too, if it is to continue to attract children to our platforms. Those of us in the children's industry know this, and it's never been more vital now that kids can access on-demand such vast streams of pure entertainment from global competitors.

With such a ferociously competitive market it is important that we continue to provide public service content at scale, and this we do; annually we commission over 450 hours of new original content, with most of it featuring UK kids in UK locations. In a typical year we work with around 50 independent production companies. Even in the Covid-disrupted year just passed, we commissioned 32 independent productions, two-thirds of them from qualifying indies. And we're pleased to state that five of these commissions came from new diverse producers, building on our practice over many years of working with both small and large companies.

Each year we provide more than ten drama series just on CBBC – more original British drama for this age group than any other platform. We also deliver a wealth of factual and factual-entertainment shows, including the comedy-talent incubator that is 'Horrible Histories', and the highly educational yet entertaining 'Operation Ouch' which medics have credited as causing kids to lose their fear of hospital visits. 'Newsround' is still the only daily TV and online news service for UK children. 'Blue Peter' remains a centrepiece of our output, the only weekly live magazine programme for children in the UK, fostering citizenship among kids and issuing this last year more badges than ever before in its 60-year history (an incredible 113,000).

We do completely unique things for preschoolers, bringing Shakespeare classics to life, mounting ballet specials and ensuring everyone's welcome and represented thanks to the likes of 'My World Kitchen', 'Our Family' and 'JoJo & Gran Gran', the first ever animated preschool show portraying a Black British family. We often look to innovate and create new formats, inspiring the creative industry in bringing them to life. Drama for preschoolers barely existed before we produced 'Katie Morag' a few years ago, then followed by 'Apple Tree House' and now 'Molly and Mack', with two well-known book adaptations for this age group 'Biff and Chip' and 'Princess Mirror-Belle' currently in production.

It's a truly impressive portfolio, which is further supported and enhanced with best-in-class digital and interactive assets for our websites, apps and social platforms that deepen the engagement children can have with the video content we deliver.

Our unique funding model gives us the breadth and flexibility to take creative risks with subject matter that needs deep editorial development. We work closely with our indie partners from pitch to transmission to help deliver sensitive projects. Not many platforms would commission a programme like our 'Something Special', which requires intensive planning and support for the contributors involved. Similarly, our recent 'Newsround' special, 'Let's Talk about Periods', sought to bring out into the open an area in which many children lack information and can lead to them feeling uncomfortable about their bodies at a critical time in their life.

And, of course, our education efforts during this pandemic highlighted the value of being able to deploy significant resources at short notice, working with many partners to do so. It would need another article to cover our plans for BBC Bitesize, Tiny Happy People or Own It. These are three phenomenal free support resources for children, parents and teachers which our education team deliver all year round.

So, for me it is vital that we can continue to support the creative industry with such a wide range of content that inspires new generations of children. And we embrace competition in the form of more public service content. We welcome the additional 187 hours added into the market over the last two years with the help of the Young Audiences Content Fund, adding to the 976 first-run origination hours we have created over the same period that have helped us reach over 10 million children. We look forward with interest to any forthcoming performance analysis of the YACF-supported commissions and their impact on young UK audiences.

I've talked about how proud we are to produce public service content at scale, yet in the market now, we find ourselves in the strange position of looking through both ends of the telescope at once. Swing it around to look at the financial power of the global tech companies, and our scale rapidly diminishes.

To respond to this we have to realise, for good or ill, that on-demand is here to stay. In the streaming world, preferences tilt towards consuming higher volumes of content, but our budgets are not limitless and we must find a way to compete with what we have. And we have a lot of great local creative talent and innovative content brands that UK children love.

We'll focus on commissioning titles with higher impact that also have a local feel to them: impact meaning a combination of editorial ambition, production values or the volume of episodes created. Already we have extended runs for 'Malory Towers', 'Operation Ouch', 'JoJo & Gran Gran' and 'Horrible Histories', to name a few, noting that some of our most popular shows are also the most public service ones.

Animation can be just as great public service as any other genre, and we have great ideas and talent in the UK that I want to tap into with this very popular medium. I want to build more British titles, such as our commission of 'Danger Mouse' a few years ago.

The aim is to take our public service provision forward in a changed world, to maintain our place in the hearts and minds of UK children. We're not afraid to evolve, and I know from everyone I've worked with in the children's industry how amazingly adaptable and creative our sector is. It's a privilege to lead BBC Children's & Education at a time when it plays such a significant part in British public service content for kids, a part that has become larger in recent years due to shrinkage elsewhere. It's great to see thoughts going into how the wider market might generate better outcomes for young audiences, and we would welcome any sustainably-funded measures which increase children's access to UK public service material.

As I've spent more time in the BBC with the teams who produce our content, I have found their sense of mission very inspiring. I think this spirit carries through into what we deliver, which I hope in turn reaches each new generation of viewers. Many people have told me that the ideas and values embodied within what they saw as children have stayed with them forever and helped to form who they became as an adult and citizen within our society. To provide content which has this kind of impact, while at the same time entertaining kids and making them happy, is a terrific purpose to have. I have picked up this baton from the many talented individuals who have gone before me in BBC Children's & Education. We'll keep running with it, and we hope a way can be found to have more join us in the race. ◖

TODAY'S CHILDREN, TOMORROW'S VOTERS

PATRICK BARWISE AND PETER YORK

A perceptive exploration of the correlation between a healthy public service media and a healthy, functioning democracy.

In many ways, children have never grown up faster and never been savvier. To varying degrees – depending as much on household income as on age – they are all digital natives. But mastery of technology is not the same as understanding the nature of the content it brings (who created it, and why? Should I believe what it says?) or the issues around data security and privacy.

In an age of increasingly sophisticated disinformation, much of it spread through virtually deregulated social media, we need both to tackle online harm and to build the public's resilience to lies and false conspiracy theories. A key part of this is to develop children's understanding of two key issues. First, which information sources they should and should not trust. Second, at least at a basic level, how their online activity passively generates personal data and how those data are used and, potentially, misused.

In eight years' time, today's ten-year-olds will be voters. Ensuring their media and digital literacy will be crucial to the long-term health of our society and democracy.

We've learnt a lot over the last year. How things that seemed rock-solid can be destroyed in a matter of months – like all those old familiar names on the high street. How people can rise to a challenge – the NHS, vaccine scientists – and just how low some other people can go – the mob who broke into the Capitol Building in Washington and the online conspiracy theorists who told people across the world that vaccines would put spy chips inside you or make you infertile.

We learnt what we could do without – fancy offices, luxury shopping, frequent flying, or face-to-face meetings – and what we couldn't. Central to what we couldn't do without was public service. Public service everything. The NHS, of course, and the care system generally. Welfare benefits of all kinds. And education: we needed people who could help with useful and trustworthy information and contacts, as well as money and food banks. People who could teach us to survive. The Government moved from Austerity to Public Big Spender because we needed it.

One of the things we realised we desperately needed was real news – un-fake news – and reliable advice in dangerous times. That meant, above all, the public service broadcasters, especially the BBC, whose news audiences shot up and stayed up. We needed to know what was really going on; we even wanted to watch the official Covid-19 press conferences. We wanted trusted people to distract our children, suddenly at home, and to help educate them. Everyone agrees – in some cases through gritted teeth – that the BBC has had a good pandemic in all these ways.

What's surprising is that anyone should find this remotely remarkable. The BBC, more than any other broadcaster – even the other PSBs (Channel 4, ITV and Channel 5) – has explicit public purposes: a mission that goes way beyond the profit-maximising business of pure commercial broadcasting. Its public purposes are an integral part of its contract with the nation – the Charter and the funding deal – and the basis for its regulation by Ofcom.

The BBC doesn't have to be dragged kicking and screaming to sign up to its public purposes. Even at its foundation in 1922 as a commercial business to drive the take-up of radio, its mission under John Reith was to inform, educate and entertain. Ninety-nine years later, that mission and the associated public service values and culture remain.

It has always invested in high-quality, original British content for children, especially younger children. (As suggested by its nickname, 'Auntie', it is a bit more comfortable with the under-sevens than with tweens and teens). It produces a mass of 'fresh, live and local' programmes for children, covering everything from wildlife to drama. In 2020, in response to the school closures, it increased production of more focused material aligned to the national curriculum.

Underlying the BBC's mission to inform, educate and entertain people of all ages across the UK is its role as guardian of a principle at the heart of our democracy: the need for social cohesion to maintain a consent that keeps things working without coercion.

We've just seen the potential consequences when that breaks down. The January 6th storming of the US Capitol showed what happens when a country is bitterly divided by contrasting beliefs. In this case, between those who believed Joe Biden won the 2020 presidential election fairly and those who believed it was stolen from Donald Trump through an elaborate fraud.

The Big Steal was a lie, but tens of millions of Americans believed it, including a majority of the 74 million who had voted for Trump. Tens of millions still do and many are armed and angry. This marks an unimaginable divide that may yet make the country ungovernable. It has already fallen behind Argentina and Mongolia in the global ranking of political rights and civil liberties compiled by democracy watchdog Freedom House, with a score of 83 points out of a possible 100, on a par with Croatia, Panama and Romania. In 2010, it scored 94.[1]

The underlying US problem of not trusting government pre-dates Trump and Biden. It's rooted in American history: its federal structure, its deep racial divides, its religiosity, its gun culture, its romanticisation of self-sufficiency and all that. But above all, its media landscape.

Unlike the BBC, America's PSBs – PBS and NPR – were launched only after the commercial broadcasters were well established. They have never achieved the scale and impact of our PSBs. The US market is therefore dominated by commercial broadcasters who have no public service remit and are only minimally regulated by the Federal Communications Commission.

US broadcast regulation was not always quite so light touch. In 1949, the Democrat-controlled FCC introduced what became known as the Fairness Doctrine, which required broadcasters to provide adequate coverage of important political issues and to ensure that this coverage fairly represented opposing views.

From 1969, however, President Nixon (who also weakened and fragmented PBS by cutting its funding and forcing it to devolve most of its budget to local stations) and other Republicans began attacking the broadcast networks, especially their coverage of the Vietnam War. In terms strikingly similar to some of today's right-wing attacks on the BBC, Vice President Spiro T. Agnew complained that TV network news commentators and producers "live and work in the geographical and intellectual confines of Washington DC or New York City [...] read the same newspapers [...and] talk constantly to one another [...] As with other American institutions, perhaps it is time that the networks were made more responsive to the views of the nation and responsible to the people they serve."[2]

The Republicans never got control of the established TV networks' news. But, in 1987, under President Reagan, the FCC repealed the Fairness Doctrine, opening the door for the launch of Fox News and MSNBC in 1996, CNN in 1980, and the growth of right-wing 'shock jock' radio. US broadcast news has been largely partisan ever since, with audiences choosing sources that reinforce their views and largely avoiding those that do not. The resulting divisions are even greater today because of social media. At the same time, organisations such as the Media Research Center (also set up in 1987) constantly monitor and attack the 'liberal mainstream media'.

For the last four years, until this January, the US Department of Education has been headed by Betsy de Vos, a fiercely right-wing, Catholic, billionaire Trump appointee who doesn't really believe in state education. She did nothing to resolve the economic, racial and religious divides that created a country with some of the Western world's best-educated people – and some of its most astonishingly ignorant.

In the 21st Century, the American media landscape has become jaw-droppingly polarised. Fox News, in particular, became central to the Donald Trump 'base', who love its raucous populism. In response, the competing 'centrist' commercial news networks CNN and MSNBC became increasingly partisan – far more so than, say, the BBC or Channel 4 News.

Compared to Fox, CNN and MSNBC are absolute pillars of rectitude and rationality. But they, too, increasingly trade in opinions rather than facts – shorter, more parochial newscasts and much more time spent on partisan comments, particularly from reliably engaging liberal interviewees, rather than a carefully balanced guest list, BBC style. And with equally lively presenters who aren't constrained by the BBC's and other UK broadcasters' idea of impartiality and balance. It's more entertaining, and it's meant to be, because American TV news and current affairs shows have to get ratings.

In comparison, UK broadcast news can often sound stodgy and look unglamorous. But – despite endless claims to the contrary – it remains highly trusted both in Britain (far more than the newspapers telling their readers not to trust it) and around the world. In 2020, the Reuters Institute found that the BBC was more trusted in the US than any other news source apart from local TV news.[3]

The current British broadcasting ecology reflects the BBC, in particular, because so many of its people were trained or strongly influenced by it and all broadcast news is covered by the same regulatory framework. Until recently, Sky News was (like Fox News) part of the Murdoch empire. But, in complete contrast to Fox News, its coverage has always been impartial. The UK regulation of broadcast news is, we think, by far the biggest reason for this difference.

We would argue that the broad UK consensus about the facts, largely driven by our impartial broadcast news, is an important reason why, even after Brexit, and despite the growth of social media and the continuing influence and agenda-setting of our highly politicised newspapers (dominated by those leaning to the right[4]), we don't have societal divides on the same scale as in the USA.

Recent academic research from the University of Zürich confirms this. The researchers looked at the factors that make nations more resilient or vulnerable to disinformation and false conspiracy theories – one of the curses of the 21st century even before Covid-19. One of the five key factors they found is the presence of public service broadcasting at scale because "in countries with wide-reaching public service media, citizens' knowledge about public affairs is higher compared to countries with marginalised public service media". The UK scraped into the most resilient group, led by the Nordics. People in Southern Europe (Spain, Italy, Greece) were more credulous. But the USA was in a category of its own, with a population "particularly susceptible to disinformation campaigns".[5]

Of course, this isn't just about media ecology, it also reflects other aspects of American exceptionalism.[6] But it's hard to see how the polarisation of US broadcast news since the repeal of the Fairness Doctrine has not been one of the biggest drivers of the polarisation of US society.

So, we're different from the USA, and the PSBs are a key part of that difference, part of the safeguard against a more polarised society. But that doesn't mean it couldn't happen here. In fact, it already is happening here, meaning that the development of social divides based on red-button emotionally-based narratives, conspiracy theories and disinformation generally is gaining ground. Ideas that once seemed mad and marginal in the David Icke sense are now believed by significant numbers in the UK.[7] The argument of our recent book, The War Against the BBC, is that the BBC is under sustained attack now, just when we, as a nation, need it and the other PSBs (and impartial broadcast news) more than ever.

The plan for this attack was set out by Dominic Cummings – yes, that Dominic Cummings – as long ago as 2004[8] and it's clearly and ruthlessly argued, with no pretence of a motivation other than party political advantage. It's based on an approach developed by American political strategists who Cummings, unlike most Brits, had studied closely. Back in 2004, he argued, among other things, for constant scrutiny and

CHILDREN'S MEDIA FOUNDATION

undermining of the BBC (check it out; it's happened and is still happening[9]) and for a British version of Fox News. And that, or something much closer to it than we've seen before, is about to happen too with the launch of GB News and News UK TV – part of the Murdoch empire that gave the world Fox News.

At a time of increasing real content and distribution costs (thanks to the US streamers like Netflix), the 2010 Coalition and 2015 Conservative governments imposed the deepest ever funding cuts on the BBC that meant its real (after inflation) public funding had already fallen by 30% from 2010 to 2019. Current attacks might see it fall still further. This government is exceptionally hostile to the BBC and appears to want to bring it to heel, to make it self-censor when reporting anything the government is seriously sensitive about.

What does all this all mean for children and their education and values? In divided societies, children learn to hate the 'other' community – Jews, Catholics or Protestants, Muslims, Democrats or Republicans, blacks or whites – at an early age. We're arguing that public service media are at the heart of countering these dangers by fostering social cohesion and the development of a tolerant, well-informed, less credulous nation where all the talents get developed. So, we need strong, properly funded public service media. And we also have to put media literacy on the curriculum to avoid ending up like the USA, especially given children's reliance on social media.

The UK national press is acknowledged as the most raucously partisan in Europe.[10] The PSBs serve as a bulwark against their biases (which is why the papers falsely accuse the BBC, in particular, of bias every day!). Accurate, impartial trusted broadcast news means that we have at least a chance of sharing the same facts and of children seeing, hearing or reading them – or hearing them discussed. If part of raising a media literate nation is the output of PSBs (and particularly the BBC) then another is providing children with the tools to understand and decode the tsunami of media (including social media) information that surrounds them from the moment they start to watch, listen and read!

Who remembers the high-minded ambition, now largely abandoned, to teach 'civics' – the basics of British public life and institutions and how you engage with them – in schools? And who remembers the efforts of the 1960s and 1970s to teach children to 'decode' advertising – to make them less vulnerable to the 'Hidden Persuaders'? We need to revisit these initiatives and update them for the 21st Century.

In 2019, the DCMS Select Committee recommended exactly that, saying that digital literacy should be a fourth pillar of education, alongside reading, writing and maths. Reasonable people may differ on how far to take this: basic literacy and numeracy are surely even more important than – and a precursor to – media and digital literacy. But it's disappointing that the Government, in its response, claimed that digital literacy was already being adequately covered in schools and by non-governmental initiatives so there was no need to do anything else.[11] We hope the new APPG for Media Literacy, established in November 2020, will manage to push it out of such complacency.[12]

Look at vox pops of conspiracy theory pedlars – they aren't just old men with tinfoil hats – and ask yourself how that happened. They often say proudly that they've done their own research, and you wonder what the process really was and how the next generation can learn to distinguish fake news from real in their own time. How will they learn to follow leads that don't just go down those QAnon-style cyber rabbitholes?

Young people's media consumption patterns are established earlier and earlier and are increasingly hard for parents to police. Between maintaining a national group of world-leading, competing public service broadcasters that supply accurate news and horizon-expanding programming, and building an education system intent on developing media and digital literacy, we can turn Gen Z into Gen Resilience – if anything, more resilient than us oldies. They'll thank us for it. ⊙

References

[1] Charlie Mitchell, 'US falls behind Mongolia in Freedom House league of civil liberties', The Times, 25 March 2021, https://www.thetimes.co.uk/article/us-falls-behind-mongolia-in-freedom-house-league-of-civil-liberties-nhkzsl9xf.

[2] Spiro T. Agnew, speech to the midwest regional meeting of the Republican Party, Des Moines, Iowa, 13 November 1969.

[3] Nic Newman, 'Digital News Report 2020', Reuters Institute for the Study of Journalism, Oxford University, 2020, page 88.

[4] The Sun, Mail, Express and Telegraph ('SMET' for short).

[5] https://blogs.lse.ac.uk/medialse/2020/04/08/why-resilience-to-online-disinformation-varies-between-countries

[6] Kurt Andersen's 'Fantasyland: How America Went Haywire' is a good guide https://www.penguinrandomhouse.com/books/209776/fantasyland-by-kurt-andersen/

[7] https://www.theguardian.com/commentisfree/2018/nov/25/populism-and-the-internet-a-toxic-mix-shaping-the-age-of-conspiracy-theories

[8] https://www.theguardian.com/politics/2020/jan/21/mortal-enemy-what-cummings-thinktank-said-about-bbc

[9] For instance in the repeated relaunches of, and publicity for, #DefundTheBBC 'grassroots' (or, we think, 'Astroturf') campaign in the Daily Express and elsewhere. See 'The War Against the BBC', Chapter 14.

[10] https://www.pewresearch.org/global/wp-content/uploads/sites/2/2018/05/PJ_2018.05.17_Media-Politics-Western-Europe_Fact-Sheet_UK.pdf

[11] House of Commons Digital, Culture, Media and Sport Committee, Disinformation and 'Fake News': Final Report: Government Response to the Committee's Eighth Report of Session 2017-19, HC 2184, 9 May 2019, pages 19-21, https://publications.parliament.uk/pa/cm201719/cmselect/cmcumeds/2184/2184.pdf.

[12] https://www.thestudentview.org/all-party-parliamentary-group-for-media-literacy/.

PUBLIC SERVICE NEWS FOR YOUNG PEOPLE: WHERE NEXT?

WARREN NETTLEFORD

A consideration of the challenges faced in engaging young audiences with news and current affairs, and the need for vision, ambition and innovation to do it successfully, written by someone who has done just that.

When stood before the teenagers, I began to understand the scale of the problem. I was back at my old school, Bishop Milner Catholic College in Dudley, there for the day running a series of sessions to encourage teenagers to consider careers in journalism. I had asked the class of 14- and 15-year-olds how many of them had watched the news on TV or listened on radio the previous evening. Of the 28, one slowly, meekly raised their hand. The shame.

I asked my former history teacher later that day if she was surprised that the figure was so low. Not remotely, it turned out. "Compared to your day, Warren, teenagers now can watch what they want, when they want – they haven't got to sit and see the news with their parents." All of this, of course, is only a problem if you think public service news is important.

I really believe we should care about public service news for young people. Communication and the sharing of information shapes our society. If we believe the values of democracy, transparency, accountability openness and freedom, framing these ideas through informative and impartial news content is vital to ensure that young people are sufficiently equipped to make sense of the world for themselves. Without it, I believe that we'll all be poorer. It's why I decided that I wanted to do something about this issue, other than just write long essays about it. I'll tell you a bit more about what I've done to make changes in the industry shortly.

Although only a snapshot in one community, I found the response from students I met that day instructive. Who knows about the level of interest that those teenagers generally had in the news? But the fact was, even when further pushed to reveal the current news stories and headlines, they were not informed. Maybe if they'd seen more news headlines or stories, perhaps their interest could have been stirred? On that day I wasn't able to tell.

'My day' was 20 years prior to the students I met that morning. Now in my 30s, having worked in TV news for more than ten years as a reporter, I deliver news stories to mass audiences primarily on national television. For a long time, perhaps even since the first BBC television broadcast in 1936, there has been the assumption that national broadcasts are the most efficient way of transmitting information to mass audiences. Until the advent of the internet and smart phones, this assumption was true. But not anymore.

But none of this should be new to you. You're probably reading this on your phone, tablet or other smart device after all. But the ongoing battle as to how younger viewers can be reached with public service news content is becoming more important. With the advent of the 'attention economy', where the amount of time we scroll or click is translated into hard cash for digital companies, the delivery of public service news to younger audiences is facing a series of challenges.

Why we should care

According to Ofcom's 2019 news consumption survey, fewer teenagers and young people are watching TV news than ever before. Over 65s watch 33 minutes of TV news each day, but 16–23-year olds only watch 2 minutes. The Government's 2019 Cairncross review into sustainable journalism had some important revelations. For 16–24-year olds, Facebook is now their most important news source. They also found "the major public service news broadcasters do not communicate news to young people in a language that they can relate to, or on the platforms where they spend their time." We also know that young adults watch more than an hour of YouTube content every day. All of these findings were from before the global Covid-19 pandemic. Since lockdown in March 2020, the amount of time people spend on Facebook has increased by 23% according to the Interactive Advertising Bureau. And so, there are two battles – one for public service media to produce content that young people want to watch and engage with, and simultaneously a technological battle for the attention of young people to consume content, any content.

For advocates of public service news media, the inherent idea that this content is of value because we've done it before isn't enough.

I want you to stay with me whilst I explore areas which I believe are in need of more in-depth research, policy and reform to ensure that public service news media for young people can be relevant and a force for the public good.

The new grammar?

As the battle for attention gathers pace, honing the form and grammar to reach audiences is becoming ever more relevant. In Ofcom's 2020 survey of news consumption, 42% of those aged between 12 and 15 (in this sample) cited the news being 'too boring' as the reason for not engaging on any platform. That's up from 40% in 2019. It's at this point I should admit the skin in the game that I have here.

In November 2019, my great friend and collaborator Seth Goolnik and I created a new youth news political service specifically to tackle this problem. Like another famous political agreement, 'The Deal' was struck in an Islington restaurant over lunch: young people centre stage in creating the programmes and delivered in a style that would appeal to them.

Launching during the then General Election campaign, our daily news programme '*Need To Know*' had immediate success, with a million engaged viewers a week, 80% of them under the age of 25. It was broadcast exclusively on the social network Snapchat, a place where young people spend a lot of their time. We were nominated for a Press Gazette Award for innovation and recently won the 2021 Royal Television Society Award for Journalism, beating both the BBC and CNN in the final run off. My own impartiality is tested here by saying that it was quite a remarkable achievement. But our own efforts helped to shine a light on the industry and public service news for young people as a result.

I don't think that our success was a fluke; it was because we had a vision, clarity of purpose and we understood where public service news media has been making mistakes. To be clear, it's not that UK news providers haven't tried to reach young audiences – BBC News, ITN, and Sky all have plenty of presence on social media – it's that when they do, they aren't ambitious enough. I think there are three main reasons why the major broadcasters haven't been hugely successful.

The tone of British news has barely changed since the days of the BBC at Alexandra Palace. Sure, maybe they now stand instead of sit and edgily pop the top button on their shirts but, for the most part, it's the same austere delivery it's always been. Oxford University's 2019 study How Young People Consume News, found young people don't want the news to be what you 'should' know, but what's 'useful, interesting, and fun' to know. News providers need to shake off the superiority and find ways to speak to young people without preaching; yes, that means humour, but it doesn't mean crowbarring youth acronyms into content.

Public service news media providers in the UK are trying to reach young audiences, putting their reports on TikTok, Snapchat, Instagram and Facebook, but it's the 'putting' that's the problem. Most of time when a news broadcaster puts content on social media, it's just exactly what they just put on TV with, at best, a dodgy 9:16 crop and a 'yoof' voice-over. Research by Snapchat shows the average attention span on social media is five seconds, roughly the time it takes for traditional TV journalists to clear their throats. Broadcasters need to forget replication and build a whole new grammar of highly concentrated storytelling, using everything from eye catching graphics to split screens, if they really want to succeed on social.

Looking more widely and taking in other news providers on social media channels the big mistake many news organisations make is to bundle 'woke' and activism together in the hope that this will appeal to younger people. I'd say this isn't about bleeding hearts but active minds. At its worst, 'woke' culture can just be as preachy as the news broadcasts young people are currently avoiding. On the other hand, studies show young people want the news to explain how they can personally make a difference. Ofcom's 2019 Review of BBC News found young people want the news to help them engage with the world. At the moment it seems there's a collective industry failure here.

With '*Need To Know*' we made a decision to communicate in a way that younger viewers relate to. As I presented the show, it wasn't only about me wearing sweaters rather than a shirt and tie but also about our language, speed, pacing, humour and story selection. I was able to be me whilst remaining resolutely impartial, following the Ofcom broadcasting code; the first digital-only news service to do this.

We wanted to ensure that young people informed the content we made by driving the coverage. In daily morning meetings we'd decide on the stories of the day with our trainee journalists and then we'd all work on writing the scripts before recording the programme in the afternoon. With all the graphics and animation work, the programme was able to go on air by 17:00 most evenings. We produced a show once a day and, on a few occasions, twice, with three over Election Day and Night. It was a truly amazing experience to have made a programme that resonated so highly with viewers and made such a big splash. It was a proud moment to think that we'd made a programme that had informed viewers of the important issues that faced the country. We've been able to demonstrate that it is possible to reach young people with the stories that matter to them. There's scope for others to do the same.

A level playing field?

Ofcom's recognition in 2021 that the current regulatory framework for public service media is in need of updating should come as no surprise to news providers. In the fight for views and clicks, news producers are flyweights in the ring against heavyweight world champions. If a teenager can either click to watch slickly produced Hollywood content featuring stars and celebrities, or content from news producers with far inferior budgets and less in the way of excitement, I'm confident in predicting that Hollywood would come out on top, unless the news content was about a famous Hollywood star. There's a reason why, on linear television, entertainment shows are in prime-time slots and news bulletins are not.

At this point it's helpful to return to the teenagers I met at my former school. When asked about what they'd watched on their smartphones and devices the night before, they mentioned '*Love Island*', Harry Styles, Kim Kardashian, football videos, YouTube stars. The things you would expect teenagers to watch. For young people, the social media space is an arena where the culture of expectation is for fun and entertainment. I would have been very surprised if anyone had mentioned a Ken Burns Vietnam documentary series. Greater choice has meant that the previous principles of broadcast television where news producers could rely on a captive audience to watch their content is slowly evaporating.

Something which shouldn't be forgotten is that there's very little in the way of broadcast news content produced specifically by public service media organisations for children online. ITV have announced plans for new news and current affairs online content moving forwards; however, currently BBC's '*Newsround*' and more recently ITV's '*The Rundown*' are the two most well-known. They do produce content for multiple online platforms, but their challenge is laid bare by reviewing viewing numbers on YouTube for recent episodes. As of March 2021, they were consistently below 500 views for both programmes. Unsustainable in the long term if success comes to be based solely on views and advertising revenues.

At the heart of this is a question of identity. As broadband speeds have increased and technologies have advanced, internet companies have morphed and changed into new entities. They argue they're not publishers themselves and so don't have to face the trappings of regulation, but they do host journalism content. Whilst at the same time, the place where children and young people receive video, and specifically news content, has moved from the place which is well regulated to a space without the values and identity that have defined broadcasting for generations. Maybe it's not a surprise that some are struggling to compete.

This supposed neutrality that tech firms have towards content is constantly being tested with sites like Facebook, Instagram and YouTube challenging the posting of pornography, fake news, false political advertising and racially and homophobic content. Tech giants clearly have values, but at the moment they haven't been forced into having values beyond the areas they're comfortable with – reputational and commercial ones.

Could it be that we now need to challenge social media companies to realise that they have now stepped into PSM territory by virtue of being the default place where young people now choose to spend most of their viewing time?

And, as young people's expectations of video content shift, could more be done to help PSM news broadcasters to connect with audiences by creating higher quality content? Perhaps more private companies can be enabled to create PSM news content through partnerships and promotions, with social media platforms doing more to enable and facilitate distribution.

Better governance

In writing this essay, a colleague helpfully reminded me of a report written in 2001 by David Kleeman, formerly the Executive Director at the American Centre for Children and Media. It's a long and interesting read into how he felt there was a need for public service media to adapt and for the implementation of new regulation in the digital age to protect and support young people. The report held up the BBC 'strategic approach' to public service children's content as something which US media could aspire to and learn from. Time and time again the report reels off how UK PSBs were industry leaders due to the focus on fixed hours of news and current affairs programming each month and the decision to launch new digital channels like CBBC and CBeebies. His argument continued that because American PSB did not face such commitments, the digital age (with increased competition and technology) would create a generation of ill-equipped Americans who would fail to properly understand the world due to not being exposed to quality public service news. With American news media firmly under the spotlight in recent years, it would be good to talk to him again to see if he thinks he's been proved correct.

Looking back and comparing today to 2001, it does seem as if we are at another pivotal moment. Although young people are engaging with social media in larger numbers and with greater frequency, there's the alarming problem of trust. Ofcom's 2020 news consumption in the UK survey found that only 39% of young people saw social media as being the place that provides accurate stories, and just 35% believed they should be treated as trustworthy. That compares to 86% and 85% respectively when it comes to television news. So, young people are fairly discerning about what they are seeing; it's just that, in the areas where they are, most public service news providers are unable to reach them with real frequency.

And so, if the Government thinks that public service news for young people is important, the Government will soon have to tackle the question: What does it want the new media landscape to look like and what should its responsibilities be? This isn't a question about how much state interference there should be with the free press; it's instead about creating a broadcasting ecosystem that provides tools to enable public service media to flourish and compete. Perhaps the fundamental principle of giving PSM companies delivering news prominence on social platforms would be a start. Furthermore, creating a framework that allows for long-term investment and greater risk-taking for innovative companies too. News is expensive and requires expertise; viewers value this when they see it.

Young people deserve to be provided with the best possible news content, and as a society we have the responsibility to nurture the next generation of citizens so that they have the information they need to succeed and make sense of our fast-changing world. Providing a framework to enable public service news to thrive is an investment that could be for the good of us all.

When I got home after speaking to the teenagers at my former school, I noticed that they'd taken a photo of me without my knowledge and posted it on social media. Turns out that some of the words from my short talk had now formed part of a school meme! Who says young people have no interest in the news? ⊙

CHILD-PRODUCED CONTENT AND THE SIMULATION OF CHILDHOOD

WHAT TALKING TO CHILDREN ABOUT YOUTUBE KIDS CAN TEACH US ABOUT THE POSSIBILITIES OF PUBLIC SERVICE MEDIA

DR JANE O'CONNOR

A reflection on how the emerging findings of an on-going study investigating how 4-7 year olds in the UK engage with YouTube Kids (YTK) may help develop successful public service media content for young children.

I begin by setting out the concerns around children's viewing of YTK, and algorithm-driven social media channels more generally, which prompted this research. I will then present some key initial findings from our study which are relevant to the current debate about children's engagement with PSM. These findings will be framed and interpreted using the French cultural theorist Jean Baudrillard's (1994, 2016) concepts of simulacra/simulation and hyperreality in order to further understand the complex processes which underpin children's fascination with certain types of digital content.

Setting the scene: children and YTK

Research indicates that the amount of time children spend watching YouTube and YouTube Kids around the world continues to grow (Statistica, 2021). The latest UK figures come from Ofcom's 2019 report which states that YouTube is the most watched channel for young people and that children are spending around an hour a day on YT/YTK every day. Children in the UK (aged 5 to 15) now spend around 20 minutes more online in a typical day than they do in front of a TV set – just over two hours online, and a little under two hours watching TV.

According to the Ofcom report, children watch YT/YTK for three main reasons: to feel a connection with people similar to, or different from, themselves (for example vloggers), to experience sensory exploration and stimulation (such as watching slime videos) and to explore their own hobbies and interests, including 'how to' videos for crafts or activities.

The constant growth of available videos on, and children's viewing of, YouTube Kids has led to concerns around algorithm-driven digital content that functions to position young children as a monetised commodity (Burroughs, 2017). Critics claim that YTK was set up to target and shape young children as consumers with values centred around consumption, competition, surveillance, judgement and reward. (Abdul Ghani & Cambre, 2020). When we contrast these with values associated with child well-being in a recent UK Government report (Ofcom, 2020), the gap between the 'digitally positioned' child and the 'happy' child become clear. The well-being values, as expressed by children, were feeling loved, feeling safe, being able to be themselves without being judged, enjoying school and being financially secure – all far removed from the values critics associate with the commercial algorithm model underpinning YTK.

It is also important to keep in mind the power child vloggers and influencers have on the aspirations and career ambitions of children through the process of what has been termed their 'wishful identification' (Tolbert and Drogos, 2019). Indeed, a 2019 study found that one in five British children want a career as a social media influencer or YouTuber, taking over from being a vet or a teacher as the most desired jobs to aspire to among primary-age children.

The YTK study

Given the issues outlined above, the purpose of the study discussed in this article is to further understand the experiences of young children as they watch child-produced digital content on YTK. The project aims are to explore how very young children choose what to watch on YTK; how they respond to what they watch; and the kind of learning about themselves, other people and the world that happens in response to this media space. As YTK has opened up the potential for increasing numbers of young children to be producers of digital content as well as consumers, we are also specifically interested in finding out what children learn from content created and/or performed by other children of their own or a similar age.

In order to address these aims, we are in the process of conducting research with 20 children in England aged between four and seven. We watch YouTube Kids with them as they navigate between videos and tell us about what they were watching and why, and we also invite all the child participants to watch the same episode of 'Ryan's World' (https://www.youtube.com/watch?v=52DjgOJYR8w). This video was chosen because Ryan Kaji is a US-based child who reviews children's toys of all types for viewers multiple times a week and who also presents play and fun videos with his family. To date, he is the most subscribed child on YouTube, with 9.4 million subscribers and more than 16.5 trillion video views.

The children are asked to respond to a set of reflective questions after watching the 'Ryan's World' video, including: Do you think Ryan is a real boy? Where do you think Ryan gets all his toys from? Why do you think Ryan makes videos like this?

Would you like to be Ryan?

The section below discusses some key findings from this early stage of the research through the lens of Baudrillard's concepts of hyperreality and simulacra/simulation. These concepts are drawn on in order to situate the study within the context of our 'consumer society', as Baudrillard terms it, whereby social life and relations are increasingly governed and mediated by representations via digital technology. In Baudrillard's work, the term 'hyperreality' is used to describe the inability of consciousness to distinguish reality from a simulation of reality. He argues that as simulacra or hyperreal copies of reality on screen become more 'alive' to us than the real person or object being represented, individuals lose the ability to tell the two apart, leading to what Baudrillard famously termed 'the death of the real' (1994). In the end game of this process, Baudrillard claims that simulations of reality come to replace reality itself in human life, and the code or signifier becomes increasingly important until nothing exists outside of the system and we find ourselves trapped in a simulation of life itself.

Whilst we may not agree with the dystopian future predicted by Baudrillard, and indeed appreciate the many positive elements of digital technology and associated social media platforms in connecting people and exchanging knowledge, I would argue that there is still much value in Baudrillard's approach when trying to understand how specific content on YTK works to fascinate and captivate young children's time and attention.

In particular, the contributory elements of hyperreality that Baudrillard identifies, namely diversion, distortion, capture and ironic fascination, provide a useful scaffold for discussing the initial findings of the conversations we had with our young research participants about their use and enjoyment of YTK and their responses to the 'Ryan's World' video. These four aspects of 'hyperreality' are described below and relevant quotes from the children indicate how their understanding and experiences as consumers of YTK align with these elements.

Diversion

Diversion relates to the entertainment value derived from a screen-based media product. In relation to YTK, the content is designed to be engaging as it relates to the children's interests, it is immediately accessible – so no waiting for the desired programme to 'come on' – and it is in many ways 'easier' for children to watch a fun video than engage with a real life activity, such as talking to family members, doing homework or chores, or simply being bored.

Interestingly, according to the Ofcom study of children aged 4-12:

"The appeal of YouTube for many of the children in the sample seemed to be that they were able to feed and advance their interests and hobbies through it. Due to the variety of content available on the platform, children were able to find videos that corresponded with interests they had spoken about enjoying offline; these included crafts, sports, drawing, music, make-up and science. Notably, in some cases, children were watching people on YouTube pursuing hobbies that they did not do themselves or had recently given up offline." (Ofcom 2019: 38)

This finding was borne out in the current study with some of the children choosing videos that aligned with 'real life' interests. For example one six-year-old girl told us: "I like watching baking videos and videos with dolls." However, for these younger children, the videos chosen were also frequently selected on the subjective criteria of being funny. For example, when asked why he chose a particular video to watch, one child answered: "Because it will be funny. I know it will be funny."

For the children in this study, much pleasure was also taken from watching another child play with toys they didn't have themselves and watching a child play in an idealised environment with pristine new equipment, happy parents and fun activities. For example, a 'Ryan's World' video of Ryan jumping through plastic shapes into a luxury swimming pool with his dad was a favourite with one child and had been watched many times before. He commented: "I've watched it loads of times. It's brilliant, it makes me laugh."

Fascination was also derived from watching another child behave in a way they were not permitted to do, especially in relation to their relationship with their parents. For example, in response to another 'Ryan's World' video where Ryan's dad has to stay on the balcony of their house for 24 hours, one five-year-old exclaimed: "I absolutely love this video. I love it! He pranks his dad."

When asked why he likes Ryan, one child responded simply: "Because I like his smile," and another said: "He looks like a kind boy," indicating the importance of an amiable, accessible virtual 'friend' presenter for very young viewers of YT/YTK.

Distortion

This relates to the ways in which child-produced content on YTK is different from the 'reality' of childhood as a lived experience for the vast majority of children; it is, in a sense, a curated version of real life – shinier and more fun. 'Ryan's World' encapsulates this through his constant receiving and unboxing of new toys – usually something that only happens on birthdays and special celebration days for most children. Ryan never has to share or play with old, hand-me-down or tatty toys, his parents and siblings are always in a good mood and focused on having child-centred fun, and they often as a family take (sponsored) trips to fun places, such as Disneyland, where they don't have to queue or wait their turn and Ryan gets to do and have everything he wants.

The attraction of this distorted, ideal version of childhood is expressed by the children in the following examples:

Q: Why do you like Ryan?
4-YO: Because he's perfect
Q: Does Ryan ever feel sad about anything?
5-YO: No

Interestingly some of the children demonstrated a surprisingly sophisticated understanding of the commercial nature of the YTK platform as clear in the following exchange in response to the 'Ryan's World' video:

Q: Why does Ryan make these videos?
5-YO: So he can get money.
Q: How does that work?
5-YO: So people ascribing [sic] to his channel. The money goes into his mum and

dad's bank account.

There was some confusion among the children as to where Ryan got his toys from, with none of the children showing understanding that the toy companies give Ryan the toys for free so he can market them on his channel. One child claimed that: "He [Ryan] helps to make them", another told us: "He creates every toy." One girl thought he bought the toys using the money he makes from YTK: "He gets them from his money in YouTube" and a four-year-old boy used his existing knowledge of where new toys come from when he told us that "his [Ryan's] mum and dad buy them from the shop."

The distorted reality of Ryan's on-screen life was not always completely approved of by the children either, raising the issue of the extent to which even very young children are 'taken in' by the commercialised culture of the content they watch. For example, in response to the question 'Would you like to be Ryan?', one child answered: "A little bit, because he's got a mansion. But he's got too many toys. He's got like a million! He keeps making more Ryan toys, more and more."

And another commented: "Nope, because he spends a lot of money on his toys and not on more important things."

Capture

This element refers to the capturing of the viewer's attention of the simulation of reality presented to them on screen and can be used in the context of YTK to describe the power of algorithms in directing and dictating what children choose to watch.

As expected, the young children in our study were unaware of the sophisticated algorithmic mechanisms underpinning their choices on YTK and assumed complete agency in what they chose to watch. One five-year-old explained that he chooses what to watch: "In my brain and then I can choose at the bottom" and another said: "I'm trying to find something that looks good."

It was also apparent that the same videos were suggested and selected time and time again with children making comments such as: "I've watched this one loads of times," "This is really good" and "I'm going back to one I usually watch." In this sense, favourite YTK videos seem to become akin to favourite toys in the children's 'real life', to be returned to and enjoyed, providing a feeling of comforting familiarity.

All of the parents whose children took part in this study reported that they supervised and placed time limits on their child's viewing of YTK as the children themselves were felt to be too young to be reasonably expected to be able to control the amount of time they spent in this media space otherwise. However, it is important to note that not all children are monitored by a concerned adult in this respect, and it is unknown how long some children spend unsupervised engaging with online channels, immersed and captured by a never-ending stream of algorithm-directed videos designed to absorb their attention and position them as present and future consumers of commercial digital content.

Ironic fascination

This aspect of Baudrillard's theory of hyperreality relates to the irony that although the viewer is fascinated by the simulation of reality that s/he is watching, the actual fascination is with the real object, person, place or activity that is being represented.

In relation to the children in this study, this 'ironic fascination' came through strongly when the children were asked about whether they want to be Ryan, with comments such as: "Of course I would like to be him, he has lots of toys." The following exchange is also particularly telling in this respect:

> Q: Do you like watching Ryan because he gets to do lots of fun things or do you watch because you want to do the things yourself?
> 5-YO: Me. I want to do it.

The power of ironic fascination seems to align with the popularity amongst children of digital content produced/presented by other children whom they can more easily relate to than an adult, including unboxing videos, child vloggers and toy reviews. Indeed, when asked: Is there anything you don't like to watch or that you find boring on YouTube/YouTube Kids? One five-year-old answered simply: "Ones with adults in."

Connecting children's engagement with YTK with the future of public service media

So, how might a Baudrillardian analysis of the fascinations of YTK viewing among 4-7 year olds, as described above, be of use when considering the future of PSM for children? In some ways, it makes concerning reading, especially in terms of the insidious threat that the next generation are being moulded into consumers of a hyperreal world of false realities for the profit of global media corporations. This is clearly not a comfortable or desirable prospect for any parent, educator, childcare professional, responsible broadcaster or PSM content creator. However, the usefulness of capturing the child's voice in research such as this is that we can listen to what children tell us about how they watch and understand algorithm-driven digital content. In doing so, we can include their perspectives in the on-going debates around the potential of PSM to enrich children's childhoods and enhance their well-being in the digital age.

In this respect, the most important findings to come out of this study so far are the children's enjoyment of content-produced by friendly, appealing children of a similar age and their 'ironic fascination' of the things these children do. If we reconceptualise young children viewing child produced content on YTK not as children experiencing the 'death of the real' but as children identifying aspects of others' lives that they would like to experience themselves, then opportunities open up to use that model to create content that enhances children's lives and provides them with more, rather than fewer, real-life experiences. The challenge for PSM is to find ways to build on this to devise ways of connecting children's online fascinations with real-life activities in their own communities in a non-commercial format. One possibility to consider would be to find ways of giving more children the opportunity to share their experiences on platforms such as YouTube Kids, thus democratising the medium and making the links to 'real life' stronger and more socially cohesive.

Our study has found that young children like content that is funny or of particular interest to them and that shows them children doing things they would like to do within an idealised, safe and happy environment. They like videos that they can go back to repeatedly to relive familiar pleasures, as well as new content that captures their fascination. The virtual YTK tours we conducted with the children also showed us how much young children like to share and talk about what they enjoy watching with other children and with adults.

This study highlights the importance of children being included in the conversation about how digital content is created and shared, and shows us that we must continue to find ways to listen to their voices as consumers as we work towards a model of PSM that includes and engages even the very youngest children, both on and off line.

As Baudrillard observes, "We live in a world where there is more and more information, and less and less meaning." Our challenge is to ensure that PSM content finds ways to be meaningful for young children in a world where their attention is constantly being demanded by infinite alternative sources of fascination. ◔

References

Abdul Ghani, M. & Cambre, C. (2020) 'Ethan's Golden YouTube Play Button: The evolution of a child influencer' Chapter 4, In (Warfield K, Cambre C, & Abidin C Eds) Mediated Interfaces: The Body on Social Media. Bloomsbury Publishing. London, UK.Pp. 83-108.

Baudrillard, J. (1994) 'Simulacra and Simulation'. University of Michigan Press.

Baudrillard, J (2016) 'The Consumer Society: Myths and Structures'. London: SAGE.

Burroughs, B. (2017) 'YouTube Kids: The App Economy and Mobile Parenting'. Social Media + Society 3(2).

OFCOM, UK (2019) 'Life on the small screen: what children are watching and why'.

OFNS, UK (2020) 'Children's views on well-being and what makes a happy life', UK: 2020.

Tolbert, N. & Drogos, L. (2019) 'Tweens' Wishful Identification and Parasocial Relationships With YouTubers'. Frontiers in Psychology 10:2781

THE APPEAL OF PERIOD DRAMA FOR A YOUNGER AUDIENCE

DR SHELLEY ANNE GALPIN

A fascinating research article exploring how the streaming services have attracted younger audiences with a genre that is a staple of traditional public service broadcasters.

The period drama is a genre inextricably caught up with British national identity. Through these dramas we construct an origin story for our present-day culture and invite outsiders in to come and experience our heritage of quaint countryside communities, lavish stately homes and Hogwarts-like educational institutions. These dramas take the form of feature films, many of them highly successful and awards-laden, and television series, at which the British public service broadcasters excel. Many of these television dramas achieve not only success at home, but are exported overseas through organisations such as PBS Masterpiece in the US, and thus achieve significant global attention. The most successful become part of our public consciousness: think of Colin Firth emerging wet-shirted from the fictional Pemberley landscape and becoming a nineties icon in the process. More recently, ITV's 'Downton Abbey' has taken up the baton, with its upstairs-downstairs structure and the scope over its five seasons and (to date) one feature film, for characters to become embedded in the hearts of viewers, tragically killed off, or introduced in later series to freshen up the storylines.

However, whilst there is no doubt that the public service broadcasters in the UK continue to produce high-quality drama, their difficulty in maintaining high audience numbers in the younger age demographics is well known. The seismic shift that streaming services have created in the broadcasting industries has led younger audiences to have far more choice than previous generations, meaning public service broadcasters no longer inherit automatic audiences from one generation to another. What's more, the period drama genre, which has long been a stalwart of British production, does not, on the surface, appear to be likely to significantly attract young audiences away from streaming services and back to PSM providers.

This is not to suggest that this genre cannot be found on streaming services though. At time of writing, the recent Netflix hit '*Bridgerton*' has been garnering headlines for its ratings-conquering foray into the world of Regency period drama; a period more traditionally represented through adaptations of the work of Jane Austen. The notoriously secretive streaming service proudly advertised that the drama had been viewed by 82 million households globally, making it Netflix's most successful drama series to date.[1] One of the most notable features of this drama was its combination of period detail with contemporary features such as anachronistic dancing styles and adaptations of modern pop songs. Perhaps most significant and unusual of all, though, was the highly diverse casting which did not restrict actors from BAME backgrounds to the small number of working-class characters that would be considered a historically accurate reflection of the period.

In order to fully consider the significance of the trend that '*Bridgerton*' represents, and the relationship between younger audiences and the period drama genre, I would like to go back to research carried out by myself in 2017-18, in which I explored the ways in which young people respond to this genre. The research, carried out with young people aged between 16 and 19, was designed to provide evidence to interrogate simplistic assumptions often made about the tastes of young people, and to demonstrate the diversity that exists amongst teenagers. The study was restricted to young people in England and consisted of screenings held within schools and colleges, to which young people were asked to provide their responses. All the young people in the study watched the same material, namely the opening episodes of two TV shows (the BBC's '*Peaky Blinders*' and ITV's '*Downton Abbey*') and three feature films ('*Belle*' (Amma Asante, 2013), '*The Imitation Game*' (Morten Tyldum, 2014) and '*Far from the Madding Crowd*' (Thomas Vinterberg, 2015).

The data from this study provided many insights into both young people's feelings about the period drama genre and the contribution this genre makes to British society more generally. Perhaps one of the most significant findings was the sheer diversity in the ranges of responses different young people gave to the same material. Despite setting out on the research with a hope to demonstrate that young people are far less homogenous in their tastes and tendencies than they are often characterised as, even I was taken aback by how differently the participants in my study reacted. Whilst a screening might utterly bore one set of participants, others were likely to engage enthusiastically with it. Films that inspired tedium, or even a mass walk-out, in some groups of participants could prompt highly emotional responses in others. Indeed, only one screening ('*The Imitation Game*') could be considered to achieve a relatively consistent response, being positively received across the board by the young people in the study.

Significantly, the screening that inspired the most lukewarm response in the study was '*Downton Abbey*', one of the most popular period dramas of recent years. Whilst the young people who took part in the study were never shy with their opinions, often expressing vehement love and hate for different dramas in the study, I was struck by the fact that many seemed largely disinterested in '*Downton Abbey*', which

I had deliberately chosen to screen because of its huge success and high profile in the years leading up to the study. Some participants expressed sympathy or related to the experiences of the working class 'servant' characters depicted in the drama, and others sarcastically noted that they wished they could have the problems of the privileged aristocratic characters. However, in general, I found that this drama simply did not particularly interest the young people, who were typically much more animated when responding to the other screenings.

This disinterest speaks to the problems at the heart of public service media's challenge to attract younger audiences. A drama such as 'Downton Abbey', which was made in the model of many decades of period drama, according to my research just does not have the mass appeal for younger audiences that it obviously did for the UK audience as a whole. It would not be accurate to suggest young people cannot and did not enjoy this drama, some of my participants were familiar with the drama and had previously watched and enjoyed it, often with family members. However, the relative indifference that this traditional production inspired demonstrates that more of the same is unlikely to build a solid audience for PSM amongst the younger generation.

The interest that my participants expressed elsewhere in the study demonstrates that the use of a historical setting alone was not the reason for the lack of interest in 'Downton Abbey'. One of the main reasons for the popularity of 'The Imitation Game' was its representation of the life of a historical figure (Alan Turing) and its depiction of a well-known historical event (the Second World War). Indeed, one of the key findings of the research was that many of the young people in the study specifically stated the representation of the past, or the ability to learn more about past events, as one of the key sources of enjoyment for them from watching the material, despite this genre not being traditionally associated with young viewers. In subsequent interviews, many of the young people identified aspects of the stories they had watched in the screenings that had piqued their interest enough for them to take advantage of the availability of online information sources to find out more about it. (One participant's use of the phrase 'googling up' to describe this process neatly encapsulates this process, and points to its habitual use by young people.)

For many of the young people, the values they saw the dramas as representing were crucial to their assessments of their quality and worth. One of the reasons for the universal popularity of 'The Imitation Game' was the narrative's encompassment of a variety of social concerns, including the treatment of women, LGBTQ+ people and the neurodiverse, alongside its patriotic representation of British code-breaking prowess during the Second World War. Perhaps true to the stereotypical image of the young, the teenagers that took part in my research often held strong opinions that sprang from their own personally held interests and ideologies. This is not to suggest that all the young people in the study held the same values, though. Just as wider society incorporates a broad range of different points of view, the young people in the study also demonstrated a range of different ideological positions. Whereas one group voiced vehement objections to the film 'Far from the Madding Crowd' due to their belief that it failed to fully deliver on its feminist intentions, another group criticised the same film for what they saw as the immoral behaviour of its female protagonist.

However, despite clear ideological differences amongst the teenage participants in my research, these young people typically approved of dramas that they saw as promoting the freedoms of the disadvantaged and representing demographics that they saw as underexposed in the media industry. The film *'Belle'*, the story of a mixed-ethnicity young woman in Georgian England, was widely appreciated by the young people in the study. This film explores the heroine's process of coming to terms with her heritage, which incorporates both the English aristocracy and enslaved people, and thus combines a lavish period mise en scene with modern concerns regarding the difficulties faced by descendants of enslaved people in coming to terms with the treatment of their ancestors and the obfuscation of their own heritage. Significantly, the representation of a young woman of mixed ethnicity in a period drama was just as likely to be positively commented on by young people from predominantly white areas of England as it was by young people from more ethnically diverse areas, or who were from mixed or non-white backgrounds themselves. This highlighted for me the extent to which young people were conscious of the need for diverse representation, even where it was not reflective of their own personal characteristics.

A frequent feature of the comments made by the young people in my study about *'Belle'* was their sense of how unusual it was to see the representation of ethnic minorities in this genre. What is so striking about this aspect of the research is that, despite the passing of less than three years since the data was collected, it no longer seems likely that this would be seen in the same way. The last couple of years have seen a plethora of releases in which actors from ethnic minority backgrounds have been cast in period dramas with little or no attempt to use claims of historical accuracy to justify this choice. Films such as Josie Rourke's *'Mary Queen of Scots'* and Armando Ianucci's *'The Personal History of David Copperfield'* both cast non-white actors in roles that would traditionally have gone to white actors. The latter film in particular, which entirely commits to the principles of colour-blind casting by not only casting Dev Patel as the lead character but also paying no heed to actor ethnicity in the casting of characters with familial relationships, has gone from seeming highly experimental when it was released in the UK in January 2019 to appearing to be admirably prescient.

On television, the aforementioned *'Bridgerton'* applies similarly ahistorical principles in its casting. Whilst not following Ianucci's method of ignoring actor ethnicity entirely (characters who are related to each other are drawn from similar ethnicities), this series features actors from ethnic minorities in a variety of roles, across all the social strata featured in the series, including the depiction of Queen Charlotte, who holds an authoritative position due to the illness of her husband, George III. Most notably, the first series of the drama follows a mixed race relationship between Regé-Jean Page's Duke of Hastings and Phoebe Dynevor's Daphne Bridgerton, although the series makes only one (in my view slightly clumsy) attempt to explain the representation of black aristocrats (and even royalty) within this Georgian diegesis, and for the most part simply allows the viewer to accept the characters as they are presented.

Similarly, *'The Great'*, made for US streaming service Hulu, also depicts a royal court and its associated aristocracy (this time in Russia), with a comparably colour-

PUBLIC SERVICE MEDIA CAMPAIGN

blind approach to casting. Here again, actors from ethnic minorities are cast as key members of the royal court, with no attempt made to explain the apparently historically inaccurate diversity. As with 'Bridgerton', this drama also constructs a diegesis that takes a playful approach to the depiction of history. (Despite purportedly representing the early married life of Catherine the Great, the drama is tongue-in-cheek about the issue of historical fidelity, describing itself as 'an occasionally true story').

What is significant about these examples is their demonstration of the potential for dramas with a historical setting to no longer be the preserve of white on-screen talent. Despite the diversity policies of institutions such as the BBC, which enshrines the need for opportunities to be provided for talent from all backgrounds, and for increased onscreen representation of minority groups, this genre has long been held to contribute to the maintenance of the longstanding imbalance in opportunities for actors from white and BAME backgrounds. There have been undoubted strides forward in the diversifying of opportunities within the media industry, with organisations such as the BBC and Channel 4 publishing ambitious policies to improve the diversity of representation on and off screen, and awards such as the BAFTAs and Oscars recently introducing diversity criteria that need to be met to qualify for consideration in some categories. However, the large numbers of period dramas produced within Britain have long been held to limit actors from BAME backgrounds, with many high-profile names discussing their experiences of needing to relocate to the US for the sake of their careers.[2]

Whilst there has been progress on this front, with the inclusion of more BAME characters within period dramas, until the last few years these have typically been restricted to a small number of working-class characters. However, in the light of recent dramas such as 'Bridgerton', these baby steps towards diversity, which clearly attempt to straddle a perceived need to maintain credibility by upholding an apparently realistic depiction of history and the acknowledged need for more opportunities for minority talent, suddenly appear somewhat quaint. The success of these dramas demonstrates that casting against the perceived 'whiteness' of British history can be a perfectly effective strategy, and shows that audiences are prepared to accept the presentation of a historical setting that is also representative of modern diversity.

Whilst historical dramas have been habitually subject to a felt need to adhere to often intangible notions of historical accuracy, the truth is that no drama that depicts the past is ever a true reflection of history. Every drama, whether set in the past, present, or a fantastical realm, constructs its own world, and the credibility of this will often rest on the maintenance of a consistent diegesis. Moreover, all dramatic constructions of history represent a combination of the concerns of contemporary audiences and a culturally accepted image of what the past was really like. What 'Bridgerton' and 'The Great' achieve with their self-consciously modern approach to depicting history is a foregrounding of this tension, rather than an obfuscation of it. The commercial success of these dramas demonstrates that organisations such as the BBC, which is known for its high-quality period dramas, have perhaps been over cautious in their attempts to meet their diversity requirements whilst also continuing to produce traditional period dramas that maintain an (often illusory) image of historical fidelity. If an actor such as Regé-Jean Page can portray a Duke in 'Bridgerton', why not Mr Darcy, next time 'Pride *and Prejudice*' is deemed fit for another adaptation?

As noted, I do not want to attempt to present the views of all young people as homogenous. My research highlighted to me the broad range of viewpoints that existed among this age group, as, indeed, it does amongst people of all ages. However, a sensitivity towards issues of diversity and minority representation, and an appreciation for characters who embodied the struggles of the disadvantaged was a frequent feature of the responses given by participants in my research. At the time the study took place, the casting of ethnic minority actors within a period setting was less common than it has proven to be over the past couple of years, as was commented on by young people in the study. If I was to use the data I collected to inform my assessment of how young people would greet this trend, though, I would expect this to be seen by many young people as a favourable development in the media industry more generally.

In meeting the needs of young people, public service media would do well to follow the lead of streaming services such as Netflix in their willingness to embrace diversity throughout a full range of its productions. Of course, there are stories in which specific characteristics of actors, whether they be of ethnicity, sexuality or disability, will be inflected in the story being told, and will be central to how the characters will be understood.[3] However, in many productions, it is possible to construct a world in which a range of demographics may be featured without this impacting on the presentation of the story. In many dramas, particularly those set in historical periods, the default tendency has been to cast primarily white talent. What recent developments in the period drama genre have shown is that this is not necessary, and my own research suggests that, with regards to the interests of younger audiences, this is not desirable either.

Whilst Britain is famed for its production of historical dramas, the success of these streaming services in broadening the ways in which the past can be represented shows that our public service broadcasters have scope to be far bolder in their embedding of on screen diversity. In that respect, it appears they need to 'get with the programme'. ⊙

References

[1] BBC News, 'Bridgerton: Netflix Says Drama is its Biggest Series Ever', 28 January 2021, https://www.bbc.co.uk/news/entertainment-arts-55837969 [accessed 23 February 2021]

[2] For just one example of this see actress Thandie Newton's comments in BBC News, 'Historical Dramas 'Limit UK Black Actors'', 19 March 2017, https://www.bbc.co.uk/news/entertainment-arts-39319503 [accessed 10 March 2021].

[3] See Christine Geraghty's discussion of the difference between casting which is 'colour-blind' and that which requires the ethnicity of actors to be 'seen' in 'Casting for the Public Good: BAME Casting in British Film and Television in the 2010s', Adaptation, 20 March 2020.

https://doi.org/10.1093/adaptation/apaa004 [accessed 16 April 2020]

WHY IS PUBLIC SERVICE TELEVISION FOR KIDS SO IMPORTANT?

NICKY COX MBE AND SIMONA KARABYN

How public service media funding can help children learn about the world and how the audience responds to the opportunity to engage with news programming that is made for them.

Children's TV is currently in the spotlight. Since 2006, funding for children's public service content in the UK has declined by 40%. Ofcom has highlighted several areas of concern, one of which is the limited range of programmes that help children of all ages understand the world around them.

As children who grew up in different decades, we both feel we were lucky to experience a golden age of children's television. From the moment we got home from school, until grown-up telly began, we were able to watch a whole host of amazing programmes on terrestrial TV, from factual shows like 'The Really Wild Show', 'Magpie' and 'Blue Peter', to dramas like 'Grange Hill', 'The Wild House' and, of course, a daily dose of 'Newsround'. All of these programmes informed and shaped our world view.

Fast forward to the dawn of a new millennium, and the world of media for young people – for all of us – was beginning to take a very different shape.

Now, in 2021, the way the world consumes information has changed dramatically. There are 24/7 news channels, radio, newspapers, and screens in many formats, whether PCs, tablets, smart phones or even watches, delivering the internet and social media. (The average age children get their first phone is seven and a half. That's six years earlier than a decade ago.) The world is literally at children's fingertips. Information – and misinformation – is a greater part of their lives than it ever has been before.

For adults, world events can be shocking. But our life experience enables us to put it in context. However, for children trying to make sense of the world, this overload of information is desperately alarming. So, it is not at all surprising that the NSPCC and its ChildLine service report a huge rise in anxiety and mental health issues in children.

The UK's only children's newspaper, First News, polls its readers every week about issues that children encounter in their daily lives. The current Covid-19 pandemic and associated wider health worries, street crime and terrorism are big fears in their lives, along with worries about Brexit and North Korea, and whether they will ever be able to afford a home of their own. Most of this anxiety is rooted in things they have read or videos they have watched online. So, there has never been a more important time to ensure young people have far greater access to truthful, accurate and non-sensationalist content that engages them.

As providers of children's content and, more widely, as a society, we have a duty and a responsibility to counter the abundance of fake, untruthful and scaremongering videos online with content that educates, informs and is empowering. We also need to give children a voice. Underpinning everything that our independent production company, Fresh Start Media, stands for is the fact that while children are 27% of the world's people, they are 100% of the future. What hope is there for that future if children do not grow up with an understanding of the world in which they're growing up and a sense of their place in it?

The great tragedy is that ease of access to information should be a positive development for children. But, the world of media, in all its forms, is falling short in delivering content for them that is honest, informative, positive, enriching, uplifting and helps them to develop healthy values … and in the place where they access it. Children are watching, on average, 15 hours of online video every week. Their online viewing has outstripped their watching of traditional television – which is increasingly accessed via online catch-up services and VOD platforms rather than via traditional broadcast. Kids no longer see traditional TV as something special – it just lives alongside online platforms. So, the challenge is to create innovative, interesting and entertaining content that means children make an appointment to view. That means investing money and investing in talent.

But, what are children watching online? From around the age of ten, they're taking part in social gaming, they're on YouTube, watching a lot of user generated content, on Instagram and watching celebrity stories on Snapchat and TikTok. So, are we ok with that? Are we ok with the fact that in the most formative years, when children are discovering the world and forming opinions about themselves and other people, we're leaving it up to chance what they happen to come across online?

Or, should we be creating more quality content on traditional channels, along with more safe places and platforms online, to help children grow up as well-rounded, accurately informed, inspired and caring individuals?

I'm sure we all agree on the answer!

Children need, and want, well-made TV content that feels relevant to them, wherever, whenever and however, they watch it. It also inspires them to make their own content – evidenced by the abundance of young YouTubers.

So, this is why public service broadcasting for children is more important than ever, as a beacon of the high standard of content that children deserve and, culturally, 'GB Future' needs.

CBBC remains the British broadcaster that airs and commissions the most quality content.

But, other than CBBC, which has the benefit of the licence fee to draw funds from, the main broadcasters either do not have targets, or are not meeting them, for quality original content for children – particularly in the 10- to 14-year-old age range. Why? Well, mainly that will be money.

Channel 4 is on record saying such programming is not commercially viable for them. But we cannot give up on these young people because of financial reasons. The money must be made available because the price is way higher if we do not open children's eyes to the real world, engage with them, challenge them, empower them, promote tolerance and understanding and help them to become active, global citizens of the future, whether through factual content, entertainment formats or drama.

To Sky Kids' credit, they have just commissioned another year of '*FYI*' from Fresh Start Media. '*FYI*' is Sky TV's children's news show, presented by kids for kids – their own view of the week's news. Sky Kids is not a PSB. They don't need to fund '*FYI*'. But, they do it because it's the right thing to do. Head of Sky Kids Lucy Murphy and commissioner Ian France are backing the show for a fourth year because they know it is important for kids to see the world in context, to have a voice, and to be agents of their own future. The addition of extra funding from the BFI's Young Audience Content Fund has augmented the budget to produce spin off shows like '*I Don't Get It*' explainers about important topics and issues '*Kidversation*' reports and documentaries as '*FYI Investigates*' with children around the world. Our 10- to 15-year-old team presents in-depth reports, and we make it our mission to get as many other young voices on the programme as possible, making it relatable for our audience. From reports about child refugees, debates about prejudicial school uniform rules, young people campaigning to end food poverty and children questioning the Prime Minister on issues relevant to them, we give children the opportunity to share their views, not to be talked at.

Since 2019 '*FYI*' has received 11 nominations, including an RTS and a Rose d'Or Award and won the Voice of the Listener and Viewer Award. '*FYI*' continues to grow and has evolved from a weekly news show into a trusted source of information where children know they can not only learn about the national and international conversation but they can contribute to it, too.

However, the future of the YACF, which has made much of this possible, hangs in the balance. Alarmingly, the pilot of the Young Audience Content Fund is concluding, having received around £13m less than first expected. That means, around 20 projects will lose out on the chance to secure funding. Around £27m has been spent on 42 productions since the YACF's launch in 2019 and the fund will have a further £10.7m to spend on production and development in its final year.

Whether the fund, which has been a lifesaver for quality children's content, will continue is being decided upon imminently. If they knew, children across the country would be holding their breath – as all of us in children's independent television already are.

Sophie Chalk from the IBT (International Broadcasting Trust) wrote an illuminating report called The Challenge of Children's TV when the YACF was in its infancy. The IBT works with the media to ensure that audiences remain engaged with global issues. It regularly publishes research and organises events to encourage a greater understanding of the changing media landscape.

Sophie says that children's media is rightly under scrutiny at the moment. Her report warned about the real danger of an over-reliance on the BBC leading to a lack of variety in programming and that it was crucial that a more plural supply of children's content is achieved.

The IBT's goal is that children in the UK grow up with access to media which informs and engages them with the wider world, but the organisation reports that excellent content is increasingly rare. Sophie highlights, too, the fact that online, unlike television, is not regulated and it is mostly driven by commercial considerations. She agrees that public service broadcasting has a crucial role to play in ensuring that children have access to accurate information about global issues and events.

Everybody that contributed to the IBT report said that there were tangible benefits of children having a better understanding of the wider world. Content which explains global events has the potential to allay their anxiety, encourage greater social cohesion, and help children develop into democratically engaged adults.

The IBT, Unicef UK and First News commissioned a poll of 1000 children aged 9 to 14 across the UK: 80% of the children we surveyed said they were interested in the world outside the UK, 86% felt it was important for them to know what was happening in the world, but only 9% said that they knew a lot about other countries. The disparity in these numbers is alarming.

53% of the children told us that they would like to see more TV or video about other countries for the following reasons:

- to understand what it might be like in that country (61%)
- to understand what people might be experiencing (54%)
- to understand events that are happening in the news (47%)
- to understand what is right and wrong (44%)
- to understand what animals might be experiencing (35%)
- to see if I can help (23%)
- to make decisions for my own actions (20%)

It is clear from this research that there is a significant appetite amongst children for information about the world that is currently not being met.

The report concluded that the development of video content for 10-14 year olds needed to be prioritised to provide them with more regulated, curated information about global issues – that they clearly had an appetite for it, and are currently underserved by TV provision. That means the YACF has to stay – if anything, to be increased, rather than cut.

The changing media landscape, and the associated commercial pressures, makes children's content particularly challenging, but the IBT says: "Shows like Sky's FYI demonstrate that innovation is possible and has the potential to bring new audiences."

New audiences like these audience members below.

Scarlett, 13: "I am a weekly viewer of 'FYI' Sky Kids news. The show is wonderful to watch because it informs young people like myself about what is going on in the world. I hear about politics or world issues and sometimes I don't quite understand them myself when I see things on social media or in the newspaper. 'FYI' is informative because it explains the current events to young people my age and is told by other young people, so I relate to it. I particularly like the segment called "I Don't Get It"... All the issues are relevant and always explained so well. Another segment I enjoy is "Our World". I love learning about kids my age and seeing what they are up to. I find them so inspirational."

Ruby, 13: "I love watching 'FYI' because they always talk about so many different things. I also love it because they ask questions about things I am thinking about. All the news is for adults, but 'FYI' talks about the things that matter to me. It's great that the programme gives us a voice."

Trey, 13: "I like 'FYI' because it informs us with what's happening in the world in a child friendly way. It's a place where young people can express and share their opinions on certain topics. It makes us have a voice in politics because, after all, we are the future."

We cannot give up on these children, and millions of other like them. Public service broadcasting is key to their futures, the future of our nation and the wider world. ◔

CAN A NEW PUBLIC SERVICE MEDIA FRAMEWORK SERVE THE CHILDREN'S AUDIENCE?

Photo by Levi Stute . on Unsplash

CHILDREN'S TELEVISION: THE CANARY IN THE COAL MINE

JACKIE EDWARDS

The head of the BFI's Young Audience Content Fund asks what lessons can we learn from the changing regulatory and broadcast landscape on the UK's public service offer for children and young people?

The current conversation on the future of public service broadcasting in the UK has been strangely quiet on the subject of children's television. The relative silence is rather puzzling given the interesting lessons the wider telly community could learn from the children's experience and, quite frankly, what happens to public service broadcasting when a heady combination of deregulation, lack of prominence and an economically hostile environment prevail.

Children's public service telly often leads the way, whether it's tackling challenging topics, making properly representative television that tells our stories authentically and compellingly, or finding imaginative ways to finance the production of shows that don't involve selling your home or a kidney (though don't rule either out). The latter skill has been key over the last decade or so, but generally true forever – broadcaster tariffs perfectly illustrate the funding divide between telly for grown-ups and children.

This historical inequity was compounded with a series of unfortunate events: relaxation of quotas, removal of TV tax credits, advertising revenue reductions and restrictions on ads placed around kids TV. The market began to fail and by 2018, Ofcom's children's content paper described the devastating impact – broadcasters spent 40% less in 2017 than they did in 2006, with 98% of programming in 2016 being repeats, with the BBC accounting for 87% of all first-run UK-originated children's programmes by public service broadcasters. Something needed to change.

Following some lively campaigning by the All-Party Parliamentary Group (APPG) for Children's Media, CMF, PACT and Animation UK, amongst others, a large proportion of the 'Contestable Fund' was dedicated to the development and production of children's television to try to attenuate the decline of the industry and encourage plurality within the sector. In April 2019 the DCMS-supported Young Audiences Content Fund (YACF) opened its doors, and in two short years has done much to re-vivify the children's landscape, spending £27.1M on 45 productions, greenlighting 187 hours of brand new content for this country's young people that is free and accessible to all. The Fund has also supported the development of 115 brand new projects which, during the last year, has proven to be even more of a vital resource for production communities. These projects are currently converting to commissions at a rate of around 10% (the BFI Film Fund conversion rate is around 5% as a comparison) and shows that the structure and process that a little resource brings definitely gets results. It is also proving the point that great content with a real relevance will equal great audiences – with shows such as 'Go Green with the Grimwades' and 'FYI I Don't Get It' and 'Kidversations' and others recommissioned in the extremely short time since they launched.

These projects are helping people to upskill, they are creating jobs and supporting company growth all around the UK and in a sector that was on its knees.

These are strong benefits for a sector that has an awful lot to offer to the economy if it is enabled to thrive. It's a sector that is globally respected and is being economically re-energised, which is exciting to see.

But these aren't the main things that makes the YACF important. What is vitally important is that YACF is helping restore what was lost to the young people of this country – television that is made for them, that properly represents them and reflects their lives.

At all times, never mind pandemic times, public service broadcasting enriches all lives, but nowhere is this more so than during your childhood and teens, when you are learning who you are, how you fit in and how to be. It is a cultural touchstone, as well as informing, educating and entertaining.

In the last two years, YACF has supported shows that speak uniquely to the lives of young people in this country, whether it is current affairs like 'FYI Investigates' (Sky News, First News, Sky Kids) or 'Election 21…If I Were First Minister' (S4C), game shows like 'Don't Unleash the Beast' (CITV), factual entertainment such as 'How' (CITV) or 'Meet the Experts' (Milkshake!), Ob Docs like 'Go Green with the Grimwades' (Milkshake!), the rather lovely, instructive and uplifting 'Teen First Dates' (E4).

This content is priceless. Echoing an Ofcom report, in a survey we conducted during last year's See Yourself on Screen Challenge, 75% of children reported that they don't recognise children that look or sound like them on TV. I'll say it again: 75% of young people don't feel seen or heard or represented. We should care about that.

Media is our cultural glue – it shows us our world, gives us our cultural sense of self. It helps shape our communities and informs our citizenship.

With the increasing dominance of the global commercials and the streamers, PSB's find themselves drawn to sometimes unflattering comparisons about the range of glossy content: the curation, the coolness, the gazillions of content spend. These new platforms offer more choice, sure, they can show us a different cultural tone of voice, and a producer can get their show fully financed – all good things. They also carry a lot of public service originated content that has little in the way of attribution back to the place they came from and were funded by. The streamers are noisy and currently well resourced, lightly regulated and taxed, are commissioning loads and block-booking studio space in the UK – it's disrupted the local production economy in both positive and negative ways.

But when it comes to content – telly from everywhere for everywhere – global TV, as it were, represents nowhere in particular. More content, but less that is specifically about us and for us. We should care about that too.

The YACF has been something of a game changer for producers and also for broadcasters that are seeing the value in content that is bespoke to young UK audiences. The Fund is supporting a lot of brilliant new public service content that will sit in places that are free to access, regulated and safe. It's supporting the rebirth of a once strong sector, which is a help, but it is not the whole answer – regulatory encouragement is vital to ensure that there is sufficient resource for commissioning new content and, in the children's sector, we could always do with more resource.

Fundamentally, content is what we should care most about – it's very easy for a conversation on the future of public service media to get waylaid and confused by platform chat. Great content is what draws an audience, not a pretty interface or a snazzy algorithm that gives you more of the same (which is sort of the antithesis of public service really – we should be broadening horizons, right?). Content is still very much king.

So, now is the time to talk about a future where public service content is made and freely broadcast in this country – it remains a crucial and central part of UK life and should be cherished.

Now is the time to point to the lessons of children's public service telly – how neglect, lack of regulation, prominence and resource risk leading to market failure, can be hugely detrimental to our cultural lives.

We need to teach our colleagues and friends in the wider broadcast community our lessons. Few understand or take an interest in our sector or our audience, even though kids and teens are 25% of all audiences and absolutely 100% of the future.

The children's public service broadcast experience shows us what a sector economically and culturally in free fall looks like. Children's was the proverbial canary in the coal mine. Government intervention via the YACF means the canary is miraculously alive, but still in intensive care. The canary will need further support to fully recover and fly again. The bigger birds should heed the canary's story. 🥚

A GLOBAL PERSPECTIVE ON THINKING LOCALLY

JENNY BUCKLAND

What happens in UK kids' media is watched closely by other countries. The CEO of the Australian Children's Television Foundation gives an international perspective on a national problem.

Distinctive, quality, locally produced content for children is a bit like motherhood: Everyone thinks it's a good idea.

But like mothers, it's also taken for granted. And no one wants to pay for it. Therefore, our work as advocates for public service children's screen content is never done.

The news that the Young Audiences Content Fund in the UK has unexpectedly had 25% of its last year's budget cut, demonstrates just how infuriatingly true this is.

The need for local content for children is more important now than ever before. With more and more globalised entertainment options on the table, McCrindle Research in Australia pointed out last year that we are living through a great "screen age" and that:

> "This newest generation are part of an unintentional global experiment where screens are placed in front of them from the youngest age as pacifiers, entertainers and educational aids. This great screen age in which we are all living has bigger impacts on the generation exposed to such screen saturation during their formative years. From shorter attention spans to the gamification of education, from increased digital literacy to impaired social formation, these times impact us all but transform those in their formative years."
> McCrindle Research 2020

Communities everywhere need to address the needs and best interests of the children's audience. The opportunity is not only to protect children from harmful material, but to ensure that they thrive – by providing them with positive, inspiring, educational and entertaining media, which contribute to their cultural, emotional and social growth.

When children see their own lives reflected on screen with characters who look and sound like them and live in neighbourhoods like theirs, they experience recognition, affirmation, and gain the opportunity to imagine all the possibilities for someone who looks and sounds like them. Likewise, when they see diversity on screen – and children who may live in their own country but experience life very differently – they gain the opportunity to try on someone else's shoes and imagine what it might be like to be them. Feeling seen and really seeing others are fundamental developmental opportunities that should be afforded to everyone. Providing an array of local stories and programs reflecting the full diversity of children and their lives, and all their developmental stages, is not just a luxury or a "nice to have if you can get it". It's a vital component for building empathy, kindness and social cohesion, along with self-esteem and resilience. That is the power of the narrative.

Children's content is, however, the most vulnerable of any type of screen content. It is expensive to produce high-quality content that children love to watch, and which lasts a long time in the marketplace. It is difficult to finance because broadcasters don't pay the same amounts for children's content that they pay for adult content.

In Australia, the Commonwealth Government spends well in excess of AUS $500 million supporting the Australian screen sector, over and above the amounts it provides to the public broadcasters. Nearly $400 million is provided via tax rebates (with tax rebates for television set to increase in the next financial year) with $81 million provided to Screen Australia (which will soon receive a two-year funding increase) to invest in adult drama series, documentaries, feature films, online and children's content. The ACTF is also receiving an additional $20 million over two years from the 1st of July.

These are considerable sums.

And yet in the ACTF's experience, any funds invested in children's content within that large overall funding envelope are hard fought, sparse and frequently resented by other sectors of the industry. The ACTF campaigned vigorously for the ABC to be given the additional funding it received for children's content in 2009, only to discover three years later that funding was being allocated to other areas within the broadcaster. We watched while Screen Australia funding for children's drama steadily declined in proportion to adult drama since its inception in 2008, when roughly half its drama spend was on children's drama. We can only imagine that, in the UK, someone in the Great British bureaucracy eyed off the Young Audiences Content Fund and helped themselves to a chunk of it for another worthy purpose that they valued more.

All over the world, the arrival of the global streaming giants has seen adult television drama production booming, as it tries to keep up with the appetite of the audiences who are binge watching it. It's a fabulous thing. But traditional free-to-air broadcasters (both public and commercial) are struggling to keep up with their competition and, in return, governments are relaxing the regulation and support structures that underpin them, to help local broadcasters stay in the race.

Those support structures that were once the bedrock of local children's production are falling away. This makes the production of children's screen content the clearest case of market failure of any sector of the screen industry, and all of us who are involved in children's content production around the world are looking for answers. What's the best way forward? How is distinctive, local content – content that in the UK is described as public service children's content – going to be secured for the long term in this disrupted environment?

I don't think there is a magic bullet.

In Australia, at least, children's content has always been made possible through a suite of interconnected policies. These include the direct funding and tax breaks that are available to support locally produced content, alongside the Australian content regulations applying to commercial broadcasters, and support for public broadcasters.

The sands are all shifting, but the underlying principles remain the same.

Public broadcasters need to have sufficient resources to be able to provide local content, and they must be obligated to make the children's audience a major priority. Obligations on commercial players need to take account of all the new players and operate in a fashion that is fair to all – for example, expenditure obligations for local content could be applied to subscription, video on demand and free-to-air commercial services equally.

Now, more than ever, it is vital that policy makers recognise and acknowledge the special public value and additional vulnerability of locally produced children's content. Obligations on public broadcasters and commercial platforms should be devised to specifically draw in and value children's content. Children's content should be able to attract the same tax breaks and direct investment that content made for adults does. But in addition, there should be special funding available for children's content, to acknowledge the difficult market position it is in, with commissioners everywhere reluctant to pay and invest in children's content at the level they do in content for adults.

That's why the Young Audiences Content Fund in the UK, or indeed the ACTF in Australia, are so vital. Set up entirely to support children's audiences, those funds cannot be diverted for the benefit of older audiences.

So, we need to argue for multiple things – a joined up suite of policy measures – and ask that every time screen production is considered, children's screen content is made a priority. Advocacy is always going to be necessary, as is the capacity to re-imagine existing policy measures to suit the times and consider all the ways and places where children engage with content. As this work is never done, perhaps the most important thing is that we enlist a whole new generation of parents, politicians, producers and even viewers to take up the fight and invest it with new urgency. ◔

PSM MEANS 'PERSONALISED STREAMING MEDIA'

TIMANDRA HARKNESS

The broadcaster and author argues that if everything has changed for the younger audience, then we need to change everything about the way we approach their public service media.

Only three things have changed about public service broadcasting: The Public, Service, and Broadcasting.

Broadcasting is the most obvious of the three. When the BBC first began radio broadcasting in November 1922, it joined a media environment that was top-down, disseminating the editorial decisions of a few to the masses. Like the handful of newspaper owners at the time, those who ran the BBC got to decide what the masses wanted, needed, and (most importantly) what they would get.

When Queen Elizabeth II was crowned in 1953, 27 million people, over half the adult population of the UK, watched the ceremony live on Britain's only television channel. For the first time, a mass audience could share the state occasion in real time, many on sets bought especially for the occasion.

Since then, channels have proliferated. First, the single television channel became two, three, four, five and counting. Next, satellite and then cable supplemented the airwaves, and now both free and subscription media arrive via the internet. That multiplication of channels and choices was the first change to overtake broadcasting.

The sharing of broadcast experiences went from being the norm, to the exception.

When Neil Armstrong set the first human foot on the Moon in 1969, half a billion people around the world watched it on various television stations. That's over 10% of the Earth's population at the time. The Times described it as "the first event of such historic significance to be shared so widely and known so immediately".

Today, people still share the experience of watching television. In fact, social media makes it easier than ever to find your fellow enthusiasts, whether for

'*WandaVision*', '*Strictly*', or a tell-all royal interview. You don't need to know, or ever meet, the thousands of others expressing delight, suspense or outrage over the same programme. A hashtag is enough to make you part of a movement, at least while the wave is trending, before the next big thing overtakes it.

But that ease of generating a social media response belies the fragmentation of the audience. For every child commenting on '*WandaVision*', many more can't even see it because they don't subscribe to the Disney Channel. A broadcast event can be big news in a certain demographic, while other segments of the audience are oblivious to its existence.

It is rare today for one channel to attract the majority of viewers, as ITV did for 'Oprah with Meghan and Harry', watched live by over 11 million people, 54% of the UK television audience at that time. Apart from Government Covid-19 official broadcasts, that's the biggest TV audience since the December 2020 '*Strictly Come Dancing*' final on BBC One. Another couple of million people watched the Harry and Meghan interview live by streaming it online via ITV Hub.

And that move to streaming services is the next big shift in our relationship with broadcasters.

Streaming means on-demand viewing. Although children do still engage with live TV, audience figures are flat or falling, while audiences for streaming services grow. Like so many other things in our 21st Century lives, we expect television to be there when, where, and how we want it. Sometimes, that's still live, as we don't want to miss out on something all our friends and rivals will be talking about (probably online). But increasingly, we regard programmes as products to be consumed at our convenience and pleasure. This is especially true for children.

Broadcasting is no longer the right word for media designed for a segmented audience. A personalised service, offering curated content for each individual, based on a profile built from data, represents an entirely different relationship between source and recipient.

Streaming changes the one-way, top-down flow of information and entertainment to the audience into a two-way flow of data. While we and our children watch, or channel hop, or even while we use the same internet connection to do a dozen other things online, we and our children are being profiled and our future viewing desires predicted. Even the BBC, if you watch via iPlayer, offers to personalise your content. In return, of course, it wants to collect data on what you already watch, both to provide you with a more targeted service and to add to its aggregated audience data.

Other streaming services don't even ask. They simply collect the data and then offer you further viewing that you might like. Sometimes that's because others before you liked both {thing you just watched} and {thing they're now suggesting you watch next}. Sometimes it's more broadly aimed at people demographically similar to you, or in the same postcode (which, for marketing purposes, often means the same thing).

So, what we mean by 'service' is also transformed.

It's revealing that what we and our kids watch (or hear, or read) is increasingly referred to as 'content' that we consume at our own convenience. We browse rival providers and select from menus, soliciting recommendations from friends as well as reviewers. Our media diet is as much a matter of choice as the food and drink our

PUBLIC SERVICE MEDIA CAMPAIGN

bodies consume.

For 16-25 year olds, more hours of content are consumed via online streaming or YouTube than from live television. For all age groups, live television is gradually losing its dominance to streaming on demand. The BBC no longer competes only against ITV or SKY, but against free online content, much of it shared peer-to-peer via social media.

Millions of people watched Harry and Meghan talking to Oprah, but the annoyingly catchy song 'Baby Shark' has had over 6 billion views without ever being broadcast by traditional channels. We still share cultural experiences, and news information, but we play a more active role in that sharing process, whether by selecting our sources, or by pro-actively passing on what we find, to selected friends or to a public audience of our own.

We are served by the providers of what we want to see, hear, or read, at times and places of our own choosing, on phone screens or generously-sized televisions, in our ears while we go running, or with the whole family on the sofa. And, of course, we are also served up to advertisers who, armed with information about our online lives that goes far beyond our viewing tastes, can target us with personalised ads on our personalised media channel.

All this means that it makes less sense than ever to talk about The Public as a singular noun. Academics working in public engagement and similar disciplines have long talked about 'publics', making the slightly clunky point that we are a roiling swirl of individuals and contingent subpopulations, not a homogenous mass. In practical terms, communication has always been segmented for different kinds of audience. Now those segments are so small that we may each be the only person in our tailored niche.

Today, although we still share some broadcast events, we experience the unprecedented range of media output as unique individuals, making broad choices about platforms and channels, and narrower choices from the menus they show us. Instead of a few editors deciding what is important enough for our time and attention, what we get is filtered, partly by commissioning editors, partly by algorithms, and partly by a network of other humans who pass things on.

We are a heterogenous public, seeking services that provide content tailored to our personal tastes and convenience, through a multiplicity of channels that are less and less likely to be broadcast.

What, then, remains of the idea of public service broadcasting?

The founding 1927 Charter established the BBC as a Public Corporation "acting as Trustees for the national interest", citing the "public benefit" of establishing such a corporation, its great value "as a means of education and entertainment", and the widespread interest of "Our People" in the broadcasting service. That is, the subjects of King George V, in whose name the Charter was granted.

This idea of serving the public with education and entertainment, for their benefit as well as according to what interested them, was seen as valuable both to The People and to the nation as a whole. It was intended to benefit not only individual members of the public, two million of whom had already demonstrated their enthusiasm for radio by buying licences to receive it, but The Public.

The 'public benefit' was a collective interest in sharing education, news and entertainment. Bringing together a nation recovering from a World War, haunted by revolutions abroad and economic depression at home, was a political as well as a social goal. Hunger marches and strikes reminded the Government that The Public was not just a passive audience, but a divided and dissenting demos.

Broadcasting as a public service could play a number of roles. It could respond to the public aspiration for access to the better things in life, as well as the aspiration of reformers like Lord Reith to widen that access and strengthen democracy. It could improve general standards of education, in broad and narrow senses, which would benefit everyone by nurturing an informed and engaged citizenry. And it could provide common cultural ground and shared truths about the world.

That was the vision in 1927, but those goals still sound relevant in 2021. Is it still possible to meet them?

The fragmentation of The Public, which was never one united voice or mind, into millions of individuals, will not be reversed by better media. Arguably, dissent and disagreement should be fostered, as the best ways to explore and test different views of how the world is, and how it should be. But the cultivation of common ground on which to disagree should be a core mission for public service media.

This is one thing that the transformation of top-down, one-way broadcasting into the multi-directional network of social media and cross-platform output could make easier. It is dangerous to mistake the noise of particular social media platforms for the public conversation #TwitterIsNotTheNation. Nevertheless, online interactions have massive potential for opening that conversation to millions of people who would never phone a radio station or write a letter to a newspaper.

A vibrant and productive forum for public debate is not just something that's nice for individuals to feel that they have a voice. It is important for the public benefit, for all of us, young and old, because it is as essential to democracy as the ability to cast a meaningful vote.

This common ground also relies on some shared truths about reality, and that in turn relies on trustworthy news and information providers. Impartiality and rigour have never been more important. The availability of the internet to almost anyone who wants to check a fact or figure should only make journalists more thorough and more transparent about the sources of their data. More than anyone else, journalists and editors need to check stories that ring true to them even more thoroughly than those that don't, mindful of the human tendency to believe evidence that backs our prior views more readily than annoying facts which challenge them.

The media cannot fall back on presumed authority, or cut corners on small truths to tell a 'bigger truth.' In polarised times, the media needs to set an example of constantly checking and testing narratives, as well as individual facts and stories. A culture in which more of us are open to changing our minds, or at least to listening to opposing views with respect and reflection, needs to include the most authoritative and confident public figures.

How does this mission square with our new idea of a service as something that, because we pay for it, should give us what we want? There are already calls to separate the media channels that give us entertainment, information, and companionship, from things that are of public benefit.

We shouldn't be too hasty, though, to see state provision of reliable news and civil discussion as the solution. Competition between news outlets continues to benefit the public by holding to account public bodies, businesses, and occasionally media rivals. A state-mandated body deciding what is true, or what is civil, smells like totalitarianism.

The regulation of broadcast and print media has always trodden a difficult line between quality control and censorship, and the extension of such regulation into the online world multiplies that dilemma a millionfold. Whether we see the internet as democratising publishing, or industrialising public discourse, governments should be very reluctant to limit that public forum.

Public appetite for news and for debate has not disappeared, and Covid-19 has only fed our desire for reliable information. Nor has the move online fed polarisation by dividing us into news silos and echo chambers. Researchers have found that we tend to take advantage of easy access to a variety of news sources. In contrast to a generation or two ago, when individuals could choose a newspaper and perhaps favourite TV and radio channels, and never know what their neighbours were reading and thinking, this generation tends to be open to content from a wider range of viewpoints.

In a world where we've become used to endless free content, or to freely choosing a provider whose menu matches our tastes, funding is a real problem. public service media providers have an uphill task persuading the public that a service sometimes meets a shared social need, not the distinct needs of every individual.

We're not going back to the top-down, Lord-Reith-knows-what-is-good-for-you broadcasting of the past. But Covid-19 also reminded us both that we need each other and that we have unresolved issues that need to be brought into the open. Media that can help address those challenges might yet persuade The Public that they still matter.

WHY PUBLIC SERVICE MEDIA NEED TO PLACE OUR TRUST IN THE 'LEAN IN' GENERATION

JAPHET ASHER

A groundbreaking article with provocative ideas for how public service content providers can reach out to Gen Z, an audience that has effectively rejected linear TV channels and passive media consumption.

In the early days of interactive TV development, we spent a great deal of time debating the value of 'lean forward' and 'lean back' viewing and engagement, and how to build moments of both for young audiences. The competition between television, online and games platforms for their attention was already underway. The issues we discussed then have become ever more urgent, as 12-15 year olds now watch less live TV than YouTube, and less time watching any TV programmes than playing video games. Less time leaning back, and more time leaning forward.

But perhaps the key value that will attract younger viewers back to public service media isn't leaning forward or back – it's about leaning in.

'Leaning in' or 'leaning into' is a phrase whose meaning has mutated multiple times over the last ten years. Notably, Facebook CEO Sheryl Sandberg's 2013 book, Lean In, pushed the phrase into common use in business circles, with an emphasis on female empowerment – going for what you want and getting it done. But while that meaning has faded alongside Facebook's reputation, the phrase has persevered. Now, it combines the old-school sports usage of putting your weight behind an action – lean into a curve, a pitch, a punch – with Sandberg's more emotionally laden idea of aspiration and belief, as well as the practical sense of taking action to support that conviction.

It was a couple of years ago, when I was pitching a writer on an idea I had for a Star Wars-based project ,that I first remember hearing the phrase used this way. "I could really lean into that!" he said, meaning he loved the idea and would enjoy working with it. I started to notice more and more people leaning into ideas – an expression of support, passion, believing in something. And doing something about it.

It makes sense that this phrase has become ubiquitous now. We are witnessing the emergence of the 'Lean In' generation: Young adults who have been shaped by interaction all their digital lives – click, like, vote, choose, share and play again.

This is the precise audience segment for which I was responsible ten years ago, when these young people were part of the CBBC remit of 6-12 year olds. I was an in-house BBC executive producer, the editorial lead for CBBC's websites and interactive content. CBBC was in its heyday, when both the channel on air and the online offering regularly topped a million users in a given week. The BBC Children's iPlayer had been launched at the end of 2008 to great acclaim.

We knew we were talking to a remarkably active and activist generation – new platforms allowed them to engage with our programmes in much more personalised and empowered fashion. We encouraged kids to make their own content with our brands, writing collaborative stories for Tracy Beaker, submitting items to 'Newsround', making games with our characters, as well as playing them. In 2013, we even ran a competition online to select a new host for 'Blue Peter'. We trusted kids and gave them greater control of their experiences with content. Whether we recognised it or not, we were teaching them to take charge, make choices, to 'lean in'.

But the research was already warning us that YouTube was becoming the most popular destination for children 6 to 12 in the UK, even though it was a service for 13-plus. My final task on staff at the BBC in 2014 was to launch YouTube channels for CBeebies and CBBC, in an effort to create journeys back from YouTube to BBC platforms. As this generation has become potential licence fee payers, they have drifted away from the BBC's services to sign up for Netflix, Disney+ and other streamers.

Late last year, Ofcom released its third annual report on BBC performance. Once again, the decline in younger audiences for BBC services was highlighted. According to the report, time spent with the BBC by 16-34 year olds now stands at less than an hour a day, down 22% since 2017. The largest drop of all is among those aged 16 to 19.

Ofcom's report claimed that young adult users find the iPlayer confusingly general – the core public service concept of 'content for everyone' – whereas the streamers, with their more rapacious data harvesting and algorithms, deliver 'content for me'. The BBC can't compete on these terms because, as a public service institution, it cannot track user behaviours and preferences as closely as its competitors. AI and algorithms that provide the tailored experience of a Netflix homepage aren't available at the same level of granular data detail to the BBC.

In a recent blogpost, I contended that the BBC has another way to create stronger links between individuals and BBC content. And it's through that other great area of debate – the licence fee. Many resent paying the fee. Some have bought into the false narrative that the BBC wastes public money on high salaries and overheads. But most feel, with more evidence, that the BBC doesn't reflect their lives and interests (another theme in the Ofcom report, largely expressed by users from lower income households or regions further from the southeast of England). It doesn't feel like the BBC is for them.

This has to change. After all, the BBC belongs to the public. We should have a say in what the BBC produces. For the 'Lean In' generation – the activist, game-ified digital natives in their late teens and twenties – this would come as naturally as liking a post. Rather than presenting us all with a binary choice – pay or don't pay, watch or don't watch – we need to let licence fee payers choose how to spend their licence fee as members of the BBC community. We need to be commissioners of our own content.

Imagine a cross between the iPlayer and Kickstarter. Commissioners place their development slates on the site, with target 'pledge points' from licence fee payers required to greenlight any content. Licence fee payers get 157.5 pledge points (equivalent to the £ amount of their fee) to pledge as they choose. You could spread your points across twenty ideas, or place it all on one. You could commit your funding to a specific genre you love – say, natural history series or comedy specials or politics podcasts. Suddenly, you are a stakeholder; your choices are reflected in the content getting made. The BBC can keep you up to date on your personal selections, with updates from production and access to early trailers. The content makers can engage with you and other pledges – a built-in audience test group for their ideas. You can share the updates with your friends, making you an advocate for the content and helping bring more of your peers back to the BBC.

This system could also become a submissions platform, opening up the BBC to a new range of diverse voices and ideas.

Of course, engagement with such a system would be optional. Many won't have the appetite for gamification of their licence fee payment, and that's fine. Plus the areas of greater public need, such as Children's, News and Learning, will need to be ring-fenced. And commissioners, people with immense curatorial expertise, still need to influence content choices, so a formula for input from the pledges and the commissioners would need to be developed. But this kind of approach could not only re-energise younger audiences around BBC content but it could also create far greater transparency and understanding of how your licence fee gets spent, and how much of it goes directly to content that you value.

Could a Kickstarter-style commissioning process work for other public service media? Channel 4 faces many of the same issues as the BBC with younger viewers who are central to the channel's remit. Teenagers and young adults remain highly desirable targets for advertisers. Their lighter viewing habits make them elusive and hence even more valuable – and critical for the economic survival of Channel 4 and its important role as innovator and incubator of young talent and diverse voices. Advertisers are pinning their hopes on Advanced TV: an advertising approach built around tracking users via apps across smart TV sets and other devices for the enhanced total video data they provide. If a brand can target their ideal consumer with personalised rich-media messaging via what was once the greatest medium for mass reach, there is hope.

But what if brands could see the proactive choices of viewers before they watch, rather than after the show via ratings reports? And even more than that, what if brand sponsors could become partners with audiences in greenlighting choices from commissioning slates? Imagine how they would leap to sponsor programmes effectively commissioned by the audience itself! They would be throwing their weight behind the projects young viewers care about, joining them as advocates for and enablers of the content. Brands may find that advocates for a show they sponsor not only convert into consumers of their products but even bring their activist instincts with them, engaging with their brand in positive ways too.

Youth focused brands already know the power of advocacy. Some have been mirroring the behaviours of the audience, leaning into social issues that matter to their target consumers. Nike's strong antiracism messaging, Dove Skincare's self-esteem campaign, even Ben & Jerry's eco ice cream warriors, show the power of brands to align with and even influence consumer opinion.

In their search for new ways of reaching the TV audience effectively, advertisers are likely to respond positively to the concept of viewers as co-commissioners. But channel controllers, producers and even regulators may well balk at the idea of ceding control. The issue they will have, I suspect, is not really about control, but about trust.

It requires a leap of faith for public service media to trust our viewers as much as they trust us. One of the silver linings of the pandemic has been the reaffirmation of what Ofcom has long reported – that younger audiences still trust public service media. Can we make that trust a two-way street and build a stronger, more valuable relationship for life with Generation Lean In?

After all, commissioners and content makers already spend significant money on insights from experts so they can 'listen' to the audience and make smart choices for them. Why not also let the audience speak for themselves and share in the choice of what gets made? What better way to make sure that our public service media is giving Britain a voice in the world and the public a voice in what we say with it?

The BBC and Channel 4 can't compete with the global streamers in scale, data collection or spend. But they can form more meaningful relationships with younger viewers around a community of trust. Perhaps by ceding some control, we can encourage this lean-in generation to be advocates for the core public service values of inclusivity, accessibility, innovation, creativity, and accountability.

That's a goal we can all lean into. ⊙

THE ACTIVE DIGITAL CITIZEN

LORD DAVID PUTTNAM

Lord Puttnam argues that the future of public service media for children is inextricably linked to media literacy education and the ability of the audience to think critically about the content they consume online.

In 2016, I chaired an inquiry into the future of public service broadcasting organised by Goldsmiths University. The inquiry's report was published on the 18th of June that year, just one week before the Brexit referendum. In its introduction, I noted how virulent the public debate had been over the preceding months and how our need for trusted information had never been greater.

Four years later I chaired a House of Lords select committee on the impact of digital technologies on democracy. The report from that committee was published last June. In its foreword, I also talked about trust. This time I argued that the public had lost all sense of what (and who) to believe in the digital world, and that this disintegration of trust was coming dangerously close to imperilling our democracy.

It is striking how many parallels can now be found between these reports, both of which dealt in separate ways with our constantly evolving media ecology and how best to future proof it for the next generation.

Indeed, the type of future we projected for public service broadcasters back in 2016 is now upon us. In the meantime, the UK has left the EU, Donald Trump has come and gone from the White House, and the world has lived through months of a gruelling pandemic. Thanks to this most recent crisis, public service broadcasters, and public service news programming in particular, have been recognised as having a renewed sense of purpose within our national life. However, lockdowns and school closures associated with the onslaught of Covid-19 have also meant that we are more worried than ever about the amount of time our young people are spending on digital screens: What are they watching? Who is acting as a gatekeeper? How well do any of us understand the digital infrastructure in which so much of their time is spent? And, how can young minds learn to recognise the difference between what's true, what's designed to be addictive or, worst of all, something designed to manipulate them?

What's troubling, is that we're now seeing a number of our earlier fears played out, particularly as young people (and their parents) grapple with a digital ecosystem they are poorly equipped to navigate. The lines between that ecosystem and public service broadcasters are now irretrievably blurred – especially for children, many of whom will grow up without ever learning to differentiate between forms of on-screen information, and the motives of those that promote it.

This means we need to more deeply consider how best to distribute public service media to children. Rather than adapting old models, we'll be required to invent new and innovative ways to deliver it to them. We will need to learn to meet them where they are, rather than wait for them to knock on our door.

A crucial part of all this will be equipping young people with an intuitive level of media literacy, sufficient to tell the difference between what is trusted and safe and what is not. A child's ability to think critically about what they are watching – even at the most basic, rudimentary level – will help ensure public service media does not get drowned out in a sea of online noise.

Consequently, any future we plan for public service media must start in organised educational settings. So, how do we do that?

At the moment, the Government has a tendency to focus on computing education rather than digital media literacy, but basic digital skills are not enough to create savvy audiences (and citizens) of the future. From this point of view, the Department of Education appears to be struggling to anticipate the implications of the technological challenges of the 21st Century. Children must understand the purposes of the technology they use, have a critical understanding of the content it delivers, have the skills and competencies to participate creatively, and a reasonable, age-appropriate understanding of potential outcomes, including potential harms.

The focus on computer science, rather than critical digital media literacy skills, is important because numerous pieces of evidence suggest insufficient progress had been made on improving digital media literacy in the UK. For example, according to The Digital Life Skills Company, only 2% of children aged 9 to 16 have the skills needed to critically evaluate news.[1] While we may think about primary school children as being 'digital natives', we could not reasonably call them 'critical digital natives'. In 2021, the UK ranked tenth out of 35 countries across wider Europe according to the Open Society Institute Media Literacy Index.[2]

During the evidentiary hearings for the House of Lords Select Committee on the impact of digital technologies on democracy, we heard positive examples from abroad, particularly from the Baltic countries, as to how digital media literacy can be promoted to young people. For instance, we learned that the Finnish government have worked for some decades to make sure that media literacy is part of every child's education. This has included investment in resources, most notably in teacher training.[3] Similarly, Estonia is one of only three EU states where digital competence frameworks must be taken into consideration while developing Initial Teacher Education programmes. The education strategy here is known as the Lifelong Learning Strategy 2020, which sets "a digital focus in lifelong learning" as one of five key policy aims.[4] The government supplies kindergartens with IT and programming equipment and training, and has assessment criteria in digital competencies at both primary and secondary education level.

Within the UK Government, our committee found it to be extremely unclear where the responsibility for many of these issues actually falls. When it comes to better digital media literacy, and indeed the place of public service media within future strategies for its development, there is a need for much greater cross-departmental collaboration and communication.

The Department for Digital, Culture, Media and Sport (DCMS) oversees digital policy and is the lead department on the Online Harms White Paper, one of the major strands of which is to improve digital and media literacy.[5] The White Paper also identifies digital literacy as an area that the new Online Harms Regulator will cover. However, the Department for Education administers education policy in England, with devolved administrations taking responsibility in the other nations of the UK, and this includes the way in which digital media literacy is incorporated into the school curriculum.

Ofcom has a statutory duty to promote media literacy under Section 11 of the Communications Act 2003. Ofcom interpret this as providing an evidence base of UK adults' and children's understanding and use of electronic media and share this evidence base with stakeholders.[6] They do not appear to run any digital media literacy programmes, apart from the Making Sense of Media programme, which aims to bring organisations working in the digital media literacy space together.[7]

Many bodies have called for the various media literacy initiatives to be made more cohesive. The Cairncross Review into the sustainability of journalism in the UK recommended that the Government should develop a media literacy strategy, working with Ofcom, the online platforms, news publishers and broadcasters, voluntary organisations and academics to identify gaps in provision and opportunities for more collaborative working.[8] public service media organisations should be among the leading voices in these conversations.

In light of all the evidence that was placed before us, and the issues I have laid out in this essay, I think a number of the considered recommendations we made in our House of Lords Select Committee report last June (Digital Technology and the Resurrection of Trust) would be a good place to start as we map out a plan for the future of PSM.

Our report suggested that Ofsted, in partnership with the Department for Education, Ofcom, the ICO and subject associations, should commission a large-scale programme of evaluation of digital media literacy initiatives. This should: (a) Review the international evidence of what has worked best in digital media literacy initiatives; (b) Map existing digital media initiatives across the UK, inside and outside of schools, aimed at all age groups; (c) Commission research to evaluate those initiatives that appear most successful; (d) Report in time for the lessons learned to be implemented, at scale, and as soon as possible.

The Department for Education should review the school curriculum to ensure that pupils are equipped with all the skills they will need to navigate their way through an ever more complex media world. Critical digital media literacy skills have to be embedded across the wider curriculum, and most teachers will need significant support through CPD to help them achieve this.

Public service media needs to be part of these discussions to help develop projects and initiatives that will empower vastly improved digital literacy among young children. We have already witnessed some really useful initiatives from the PSBs – just look at the value children and their parents have extracted from the BBC's educational programming during the pandemic, and the kind of resources that are now available via BBC Teach. Collaborations between PSBs and digital platforms (like the '*Channel 4 News*'/Facebook partnership) are clearly a step in the right direction, but none go far enough.

As I said when I chaired the inquiry into the future of public service television in 2016: "Public service broadcasting is a noble 20th Century concept."[9] In many ways, the spirit of that concept has been best exemplified during the grimmest days of the Covid-19 crisis, when people across the four nations turned to trusted public-service voices for reliable information, and to local programming for familiarity and comfort. However, if this sense of noble purpose is to be maintained, PSM must be supported by Government to keep pace with the rapidly evolving media ecosystem. This is particularly true when it comes to children's PSM, as young people everywhere increasingly migrate towards digital gaming, online social-media platforms and short-form video apps.

As I have made clear over the course of this piece, the first place to start in protecting the future of PSM is to invest in initiatives that will help our young people to think more critically about the content they consume, especially online. Better educational programmes for digital literacy must be established; there are great dangers involved in passing the buck from department to department, and ultimately ignoring the problem.

Beyond the pressing need for a more cohesive digital media literacy strategy, Government must work with broadcasters to think outside the box (literally!) when it comes to the delivery of PSM to young people. Imagine a new public service platform for this generation: one that escapes the shackles of YouTube, Facebook and TikTok. How we also make it compelling is an altogether different matter – but surely not insuperable!

We need to provide children with the tools they'll require to negotiate this new media landscape, and think about how PSBs can be both their compass and a reliable and trusted destination.

References
[1] https://www.digitallifeskills.org.uk/ [accessed 27 April 2021]; House of Lords Select Committee on Democracy and Digital Technologies, Digital Technology and the Resurrection of Trust, (June 2020): https://committees.parliament.uk/publications/1634/documents/17731/default/(DAD0033)

[2] Media Literacy Index 2021. https://osis.bg/?p=3750&lang=en [accessed 27 April 2021]

[3] https://www.digitallifeskills.org.uk/ [accessed 27 April 2021]; House of Lords Select Committee on Democracy and Digital Technologies, Digital Technology and the Resurrection of Trust, (June 2020): https://committees.parliament.uk/publications/1634/documents/17731/default/ (Q 150)

[4] Republic of Estonia Ministry of Education and Research, 'The Estonian Lifelong Learning Strategy 2020': https://www.hm.ee/sites/default/files/estonian_lifelong_strategy.pdf [accessed 28 April 2020]; NESTA, 'Digital Frontrunners Spotlight: Estonia': https://www.nesta.org.uk/blog/

digital-frontrunners-spotlight-estonia/ [accessed 28 April 2021]

[5] Online Harms White Paper - GOV.UK (www.gov.uk) [accessed 27 April 2021]

[6] About media literacy - Ofcom [accessed 27 April 2021]

[7] Making Sense of Media - Ofcom [accessed 27 April 2021]

[8] 'The Cairncross Review, A Sustainable Future for Journalism' (February 2019) p 90: https://assets.publishing.service.gov.uk/government/uploads/system/uploads/attachment_data/file/779882/021919_DCMS_Cairncross_Review_.pdf [accessed 28 April 2021]

[9] 'A Future for Public Service Television: Content And Platforms in a Digital World: A report on the future of public service television in the UK in the 21st Century', Goldsmiths University of London, 2016. https://futureoftv.org.uk/

PUBLIC SERVICE MEDIA: A MATTER OF LIFE AND DEATH

DR MAI ELSHEHALY AND PROFESSOR MARK MON-WILLIAMS

Based on the extensive scientific research of the ongoing Born In Bradford project, an exceptionally powerful plea for policymakers to recognise the vital importance of storytelling in how we share knowledge with children and young people and the impact the successful transmission of knowledge can have on young lives.

Culture is one of the defining aspects of humanity. This is not to say that other species do not demonstrate cultural customs, but the extent to which humans pass down traditions is arguably one of the most important features that distinguishes us from all other animals. Indeed, Joseph Henrich has argued that the transmission of information through culture is a matter of life and death. Henrich's arguments are supported by the observation that Burke and Wills starved to death in the middle of the Australian outback in their ill-fated expedition of 1861. Notably, the place where Burke and Wills died was not lacking in food and supported Aboriginal Australians who lived in the area. The problem was that Burke and Wills had not been taught the skills that they needed to survive in the environment in which they found themselves. Thus, Burke and Wills serve as a salutary reminder that humans thrive through the cultural transmission of local and temporally adaptive information.

The comforts of modern life mean that most people living within developed countries are not placed in extreme life-threatening situations where they need to find food and shelter in an untamed environment. Nevertheless, there are large swathes of our population who experience premature death as a function of the place they live. Conversely, the world's population (on average) enjoys a better quality of life than the preceding generations. In the words of Hans Rosling: Things are bad, but they are better." Things are better because humans have found an efficient process for transmitting accurate information (we call this process 'science') and have created excellent systems for transmitting information through the generations (we call these systems 'schools' and 'universities').

Public service media (PSM) is a crucial partner in the fight against the health inequalities that blight our country and the world. In essence, PSM enables equitable access to accurate information (thanks to regulation and moderation), and the transmission of reliable information is the most powerful tool that humans possess in our fight against existential crises, totalitarian regimes, and social injustices (including health inequalities).

Covid-19 has accelerated health inequalities

The Marmot review of 2010 shone a spotlight on the health inequalities that blight the UK, showing that the many people who die prematurely each year, as a result of health inequalities, would have otherwise enjoyed between 1.3 and 2.5 million extra years of life in total. Marmot made six policy recommendations:

1. Give every child the best start in life
2. Enable all children, young people and adults to maximise their capabilities and have control over their lives
3. Create fair employment and good work for all
4. Ensure a healthy standard of living for all
5. Create and develop healthy and sustainable places and communities
6. Strengthen the role and impact of ill-health prevention

In 2020, Marmot published a new review showing that the problems identified in 2010 had not improved – in fact, the inequalities had become worse. He reported that people can expect to spend more of their lives in poor health; improvements to life expectancy have stalled, and declined for the poorest women; the health gap between wealthy and deprived areas has grown so that living in a deprived area of North East England is worse for your health than living in a similarly deprived area in London (to the extent that life expectancy is nearly five years less). It is clear that the strategies implemented by governments over the last decade have not delivered the policy changes recommended by Marmot, and the geographical gaps have deepened. For example, in Bradford (the UK's youngest city and sixth largest) there were 12 wards in the bottom 10% of the Index of Multiple Deprivation in 2015, but by 2019 this had increased to 14 wards.

Moreover, the bleak picture painted by Marmot in 2020 preceded the onslaught of the Covid-19 pandemic. In Bradford, we have been tracking the lives of over 13,500 children and their families via the Born in Bradford longitudinal birth cohort study. Our Born in Bradford project allows us to monitor changes over time, and enabled us to establish, accurately, how the UK's lockdown affected the most disadvantaged members of our communities. The evidence from Born in Bradford was that the lockdown exacerbated the inequalities already plaguing our district. We found an increase in markers of poverty with a substantial number of families experiencing multiple vulnerabilities. Food security decreased and physical health behaviours worsened. Mental ill health become rife, and the risk of poor mental wellbeing was higher in the increased number of families struggling financially. Digital inequalities limited access to remote education: South Asian heritage children had less access to computer equipment and the internet compared to white-British children. Classroom inequalities increased with teachers expressing concern over the disproportionate effect on vulnerable children and children with special educational needs and disability (SEND).

The aftermath of the pandemic

In the UK, the rates of Covid-19 are now falling rapidly and the social restrictions are easing thanks to the availability of vaccines. Unfortunately, the lasting damage created by the lockdown remains. Covid-19 has highlighted the inequalities within our society, and it has also worsened the problem. Thus, there is an urgent need for a renewed attack on the inequalities that are crippling our communities. The ethical and moral imperative for action is unarguable, but the economic case is also overwhelming. Our health services were not designed for the appalling levels of poor population health that we are experiencing within the UK. Our population is suffering from high rates of preventable disease (including mental ill health) that would have been unimaginable to the founders of the NHS. Moreover, these non-communicable diseases are concentrated in our most deprived areas. Notably, there is a growing mountain of evidence that shows acting early (i.e. helping children adopt health lifestyles) is the most effective way of tackling long-term physical and mental health problems. There is also a growing body of evidence that shows early interventions save public finances in the long term. This makes sense – the long-term costs of treating the sequelae of issues, such as childhood obesity, are well documented.

PSM has a major responsibility in tackling health inequalities

How can we implement strategies that will allow the policy changes identified by Marmot? There are numerous arguments that blame politicians for ideological decisions relating to a lack of investment in tackling childhood poverty. These arguments are compelling, but don't speak to the issue of why investments are often ineffective in shifting the needle on such 'wicked' societal problems. The arguments can also be convenient in shifting the blame to one part of the system (e.g., central government) and thereby abdicate responsibility from other parts of the system (from universities through local governments to media outlets). Science suggests that the solutions lie across the whole complex system within which children develop, with everyone and every organisation having a role to play in tackling the health inequalities that affect each district within the UK and across the world.

PSM organisations have a major responsibility in helping achieve the mission of reducing structural inequalities within our societies. But PSM must harness the tools of science if it wants to realise its true potential in improving the public's quality of life. The pandemic is being brought under control because we have harnessed the power of science in the fight against communicable diseases. In short, vaccines are a fantastic testament to the most powerful tool that humans possess – the scientific process. Science is the process that humans developed to ensure quality control in the cultural transmission of information. Scientific principles ensure that the information transmitted through space (i.e., learning shared across the world) and time (i.e., passed down through the generations) is as accurate as possible. It is the accurate transmission of information that allows different groups of humans and different generations to learn the skills and behaviours that will allow them to thrive in the world.

PSM organisations could and should consider a focus on supporting schools

One of the greatest achievements of human civilisation was the creation of organisations committed to providing the information needed by future generations to survive and thrive on planet Earth. The existence of schools and universities is testimony to the importance of information transmission within human society. Indeed, the progress that has been made in decreasing societal inequalities within the UK can be directly associated with the increasing access to information provided by schools to all children – regardless of background. Once more, as Rosling put it, things are bad but better – we can create meaningful change through transmitting accurate information. This suggests strongly that it is worthwhile focussing on schools when we consider how to implement Marmot's recommended policies.

The existence of state schools within the UK provides a great opportunity to 'level the playing field' for our most disadvantaged children. The schools are also a useful reminder that developed countries have many advantages that are not yet enjoyed by other countries throughout the world. The presence of a state school system is a necessary factor in eradicating inequalities, but it is not a sufficient element. The problem faced by many schools within the UK is that their efforts to educate children are thwarted by issues playing out on the other side of the school gates. These problems were illustrated throughout the pandemic by the digital inequalities flagged earlier. The provision of educational materials through online platforms and the switch towards remote teaching was difficult for all children – but it disenfranchised a large number of children who lacked access to computer equipment and the internet (and/or did not have parents who were digitally literate).

The role for PSM in working with schools (and nurseries, health visitors, parents, etc.) to provide the requisite information for the development of skills is immediately apparent. Proponents of PSM rightly draw attention to the need to inform and entertain citizens. But its potential can be stated in starker terms. PSM can literally save lives through the provision of information that: (i) allows parents to better support their child's development; (ii) helps schools in their efforts to educate children; (iii) empowers children and young people to make healthy life choices. There is a great opportunity for PSM organisations to work with schools (we include nurseries etc in this broad category) to produce content that really matters to communities, and help provide children and young people with the information they need to thrive – regardless of their background.

How can PSM save lives?

The Covid-19 pandemic has shown us many examples where rapid communication of new information and the reshaping of cultural and social norms were key to saving lives. People have needed to adopt a radical shift in their understanding of what constitutes 'responsible behaviour'. The ability to access accurate information has enabled communities to adapt the traditional behaviours shaped by their cultural heritage. This was well exemplified by religious festivals. People of all faiths were told that they should no longer congregate and worship in the way that they had previously learned was right for them.

The media (including PSM) played a large role in communicating the need for such cultural shifts. The extent to which the required changes were adopted by communities was largely influenced by the media and the extent to which communities trusted the communicated information. Thus, it is not unsurprising that there was a significant impact on the rates of infection and deaths in countries where PSM was available and trusted. Indeed, we are still seeing the ravaging impact of the pandemic in many countries where the media played a limited or biased role. In some countries, the media continued to portray traditional religious practices and social gatherings as desirable activities. This is an understandable narrative under normal circumstances but is deeply problematic within a pandemic – as indexed by the catastrophic rates of infection. In short, PSM has proved a key determining factor within the health and wellbeing of different populations throughout the pandemic.

The future of PSM in addressing wider issues of inequality

The pandemic shows the potential for PSM to save lives through the provision of accurate information that can shape the decisions made within a population facing a communicable disease. We now need to use the power of PSM to tackle the non-communicable disease epidemic. If we are to be effective in addressing health inequalities then we need to determine what critical information needs to be supplied, how this information is best provided, and how information can be tailored for different demographic groups (recognising that an approach effective for white-British boys is unlikely to be optimal for girls of South Asian heritage). In other words, we need to embrace the scientific method if we want to ensure that PSM maximises its potential.

In Bradford, we have been developing the infrastructure that allows such a scientific approach to be adopted. The Born in Bradford (BiB) children are entering secondary school and we are expanding the cohort to include all of the children within the BiB age band. This is increasing the size of our cohort to over 30,000 children and young people and the programme of work (entitled 'Age of Wonder') will involve the 38 secondary schools across our district. In turn, this has created the *Digital Makers* programme that seeks to learn how we can best upskill children and young people and teach them their digital rights. Importantly, Digital Makers is adopting the scientific method and testing different approaches so we can learn what works best and what needs to be tailored to individual communities. The potential for PSM organisations to be involved in this work is immense – and, indeed, we have representatives from organisations such as the BBC and C4 who are committed to the ethos of PSM. We work in a building (the Wolfson Centre within the Bradford Royal Infirmary) that has a large neon sign proclaiming 'everything is connected'. The sign was created by one of our artists in residence (Ian Beasley) and captures the sentiments expressed by our poet in residence (Ian MacMillan) in his poem of that title. This well reflects our belief that artists and cultural practitioners are as important as technologists and medical practitioners in addressing the issues of health inequality.

117

The fact that everything is connected means that we need to consider the interactions between PSM and existing cultural practices. The growing body of evidence on norm-shaping media interfaces tells us that the role of PSM in saving and improving lives will be driven largely by its ability to capture the 'big picture' that considers physical, mental, cultural, and social elements in a place-based manner. Lessons learned from around the world reveal that patterns of behaviour are largely influenced by the local and temporally adaptive customs transmitted through the generations (i.e., cultural heritage). For example, in the Middle East, where 90% of young Arabs use at least one social media channel every day, it has been reported that users spend around 2 million more hours daily on Facebook during Ramadan. This seasonal increase in social media adoption is not surprising given the wider context of media consumption during Ramadan in the region. In 2021, for example, 92 new TV dramas and soap operas premiered and aired in Ramadan, and Linear TV reach in Saudi Arabia was about 97% in the first week of the holy month. Patterns like these provide insights on the interacting dynamics between behaviours, social media, and PSM. These patterns make it clear that media consumption is a product of cultural heritage, and vice versa. The question then becomes: How can PSM harness the norm-shaping ability of social media consumption to create an ecosystem for systemic change that takes local context into account and addresses inequalities globally and at home?

PSM can allow equitable access to information at a global scale and save lives

Our challenge to PSM organisations is to adopt a 'whole system approach', and consider their societal role in a holistic manner. PSM organisations could and should debate how they can help implement Marmot's recommendations. There is an enormous part for PSM to play in helping to educate children and give them the information they need to develop the skills necessary to survive, thrive, and enjoy a healthy life in the place they reside. Moreover, PSM can teach children how to use the emerging digital technologies that can facilitate access to information (i.e., it can help children 'learn to learn'). In Bradford, we have a new ten-year cultural strategy – Culture Is Our Plan – that is bringing communities together with artists, cultural practitioners, scientists and medical researchers to generate lasting change for our children and young people. This initiative means we can work with our PSM partners to create a more equal society through the improved transmission of information.

In summary, PSM has the ability to reshape cultural and societal norms in a way that increases the adoption of digital technologies and affords more equitable educational opportunities for children worldwide. In this way, PSM can enable public services to reach countries where the devastating impacts of war and instability are crippling education, and support countries where the quality of education is primarily determined by gender, religious background, and/or socioeconomic status. There is incontrovertible evidence that improving education in this way will save lives. In countries such as the UK, PSM is a necessary component in the urgent fight to save lives from non-communicable diseases, and could play a significant role in the battle we need to fight against the inequalities that are killing our communities.

AS KIDS KICKSTART THE METAVERSE, IS PUBLIC SERVICE MEDIA READY?

DAVID KLEEMAN

Drawing on extensive global research, this article highlights the challenges and opportunities for regulators and children's media producers as they prepare for changes in media habits we have only begun to imagine.

> "[The metaverse is] arguably as big a shift in online communications as the telephone or the internet."
> David Baszucki, CEO, Roblox

Any debate on the future of public service media for children cannot assume that what children are doing now is what they will be doing five years from now. To plan for the future, you have to imagine the future. And just as 'transmedia' and '360 commissioning' were buzzwords in recent years for brand extension to additional platforms, in 2021 we'll hear the term 'metaverse' with increasing frequency.

The former terms had a few challenges. 'Transmedia' was used overly broadly to mean any property with both video and a website or game. '360 commissioning' was too often seen from an anxious commissioner's perspective, not from where children wanted and expected to engage with their favourite stories and characters. This time, the roles are reversed and it's the audience – the kids – who are taking the medium into their own hands and writing the narrative.

There is, as yet, no true metaverse – Roblox and '*Fortnite*' come closest – but there is a thriving editorial exchange and digital industry in defining and building the variety of elements that ultimately will click together like a jigsaw puzzle, making a seamless whole.

Matthew Ball suggests that we need to reinvent entertainment for a generation that's never been without touchscreen, mobile, interactive media. "Today's generation thinks very differently because they're 'wired' for interaction, for creation, to participation, for marketplaces, to be a click away from communicating with their friends for shared experiences anywhere."

If young people are going to congregate there, it's critical that there be non-commercial worlds within metaverses devoted to otherwise under-served ideas, information and communities. While the foundation of public service media has traditionally been universally-available, free-to-all services, when public broadcasters don't claim space on new platforms from the start (often before access is ubiquitous), all the prime 'real estate' will already be held by commercial interests.

Who will define and create the 'public service' content and experiences? Is it children, since these are places for creation as much as consumption? What is the role for the historic public service organisations and overseers, such as BBC and Ofcom?

This article will begin to address what a metaverse is and isn't, enabling the UK creative community to be 'metaverse ready'. Our goal is to project how young audiences will navigate, discover, engage and share their favourite content. From there, the children's media industries – public and commercial – can critically assess where their IP fits and how to build thoughtfully and sustainably for the future.

What is a metaverse?

The definition of a metaverse is still evolving, with people's varying approaches reflecting the role they play in its evolution.

For example, venture capitalist and strategist Matthew Ball considers the size and dimensions of a true metaverse from a creator's perspective, suggesting it will be:

- massive, persistent, live and synchronous;
- spanning both digital and physical spaces;
- encompassing a built-in economy; and
- embracing multiple entities (array of brands, story-worlds, games and more).

By contrast, Roblox CEO David Baszucki's eight characteristics of a metaverse more reflect players' desired experience:

- Identity - my avatar reflects my real or imagined self and is present and consistent wherever I go;
- Friends - I can socialize and play with real-world friends and also befriend and interact with others in-world;
- Immersiveness - the metaverse removes me from my day-to-day, into a fully-formed alternative world;
- Anywhere - I can create and play from anywhere, across all types of devices;
- Variety - content and experiences are both deep and wide, accommodating diverse and curious users;
- Low friction - onboarding and transitions are easy, to encourage trying new things;
- Economy - I can acquire goods or services entirely within the metaverse, and those

who provide them are paid for their efforts; and

• Trust and civility - the metaverse is welcoming, equitable, diverse and kind – and fully respects GDPR, COPPA and other youth safety regulations.

Dubit Founder Matt Warneford adds insight into the concept's humanity: "The metaverse is defined by its ability to satisfy our need to be around other people – live and 'in person'. Much of the internet is made up of lonely experiences; we keep in contact, but we don't feel together. Spending time in the metaverse feels more like reading in a coffee shop or hanging out in the mall with friends. There's a long way to go: the technologies to enable the fullest version of this are as far from today's capabilities as we are from the 1990s internet. There's no question, though, that a growing share of our time will be spent within virtual spaces and with virtual goods – for education, work, health, politics and leisure."

Why should I care?

In the last 20+ years, the media environment has become increasingly fragmented across multiple devices and platforms. Where once we had fewer than a dozen channels of television, now there are hundreds of linear channels, dozens of OTT VOD platforms, YouTube and other video sites. That's just for 'TV'.

Game and mobile app stores have millions of titles. Content discovery has become incredibly difficult: in Dubit's Trends studies, upwards of 60% of 2-15 year olds said they often or sometimes have trouble finding their next "favourite thing".

At present, content discovery is like being given a paper map and told to find a specific location and the best way to get there. A metaverse will be more like navigation software, with places and routes connected beneath the surface by prompts, algorithms and AI to plot your route and recommend other places of interest. Alternatively, it may be more like a 'tesser' or Harry Potter-esque 'apparation', enabling instant transport from place to place.

The benefit of being immersive, always-on and persistent is that your 'stuff' – avatars, skins, emotes, weapons, currency and other resources – will stay with you as you play, build, socialise, leave and return. Different platforms of a particular IP – its 'transmedia' elements – should be interconnected and seamless within the metaverse. The same applies across devices, such that a player could lay down a game controller and pick up a smartphone without interrupting engagement.

There's another, bigger reason to care about the metaverse: it provides an opportunity to create a world essentially from the ground up. What kind of choices will we make?

In the US, commercial television was launched long before the country realised something was missing, and introduced public TV. By contrast, in the UK, the BBC was well established before commercial services were allowed, and even then many had public service mandates. The effects of these 180-degree different histories echo to this day not just in television, but across the countries' approach to media.

Tim Berners-Lee, a creator of the World Wide Web, is optimistic about the future of the internet, with youth in the lead: "Hopefully there will be a cohort of young people who realise that the world does not have to be the way it is." This can only happen, though, he notes, if we commit to global equity of access and resolving online toxicity: "Today, we're seeing just a fraction of what's possible. Because while we talk about a generation of 'digital natives', far too many young people remain excluded and unable to use the web to share their talents and ideas."

Is the metaverse for kids, though?

Like any universe, there will be parts of the metaverse that are kid-appropriate and there will be adults-only neighborhoods. Without question, though, children and teens are already kickstarting the metaverse in their digital play and socialising.

This isn't surprising: who better than young people could benefit from a coherent, connected, easy-to-navigate world of play, creation and learning? Kids immediately understand the metaverse concept – a nearly-boundless space where they're free to pursue their favorite brands, stories and characters in all their variations.

Youth are driving the explosive growth of Roblox, currently the nearest approximation to a metaverse. The platform was already popular pre-pandemic, but Roblox has become young people's top space for everything from little kids' birthday parties to adolescents' live concerts, while they've been prevented from being with friends in person.

As 'down on the corner' shifted to 'up on the server', kids and teens 'hacked' platforms not designed for them, like Zoom and Discord, adapting them to their needs for connection and engagement. They're building their own metaverse piece by piece, solving with tech for the challenges in their lives.

In children's lives today, everything competes with everything. Netflix CEO Reed Hastings says, "We compete with '*Fortnite*', and we lose." It's not "do I watch this channel or this one" but "where can I best get what I need right now – a game or a video, on my phone or my TV, alone or with friends, by consuming or creating?"

With young people leading the way, the metaverse will have massive responsibility for safety, following both the letter and spirit of laws, regulations and terms of service. Communication and social play being inherent to immersive worlds, this creates a design and development challenge to have foolproof identifiers, persistent throughout the metaverse, carrying a player's permissions (including age) to enable access to appropriate areas and leveling modes of connection and communication.

Roblox CEO Baszucki believes that users will do their part to create a respectful citizenry:

> "People will know they have a physical identity and a digital identity, Just as people that are very facile with books and videos and balancing them, we're optimistic they will be with the metaverse as well. We're not so dystopian in our vision relative to maybe some science fiction. We think people will be able to balance this and use it in a positive way. We think it will be an integral part of learning and working. Just another tool side by side with video and books and other forms of communication."

A metaverse needs an economy (see below) that may well merge real-world currency, cryptocurrency, NFTs (Non-Fungible Tokens) and in-world 'money'. These physical and digital worlds collided recently, when Epic Games paid complainants in a class-action lawsuit over 'loot boxes' with a mix of Fortnite V-Bucks, Rocket League credits and US dollars.

One metaverse or many?

Ready Player One and its OASIS notwithstanding, it seems unlikely that any one metaverse will emerge for a long time. The resources needed – servers, creative development, business relations, moderation – are larger than even current behemoths (Amazon, Apple, Facebook, Microsoft) could support. Corporate competitiveness will likely mean development of multiple immersive worlds, to some extent defeating the 'seamless' purpose of a metaverse, though, like drops of mercury on a plate, these stand-alone worlds may ultimately connect or merge.

As noted, there isn't a complete metaverse as yet. TechCrunch calls our current state the multiverse, where an array of virtual worlds "function almost like new countries in our society, countries that exist in cyberspace rather than physical locations but have complex economic and political systems that interact with the physical world." Each of the biggest platforms – Facebook, 'Fortnite', 'Minecraft', Core, and Roblox – incorporates major elements of what a metaverse will be.

Will these grow independently as worlds competing for our attention and commerce? Will tendrils of the multiple worlds connect, forming a virtual 'union' throughout which players can easily commute? Will one of the massive tech companies acquire enough of them to create a *de facto* behemoth metaverse?

Roblox: The proto-metaverse

Based on the definitions above, we can see the seeds of the metaverse in Roblox. It isn't a game, but a multiplayer game platform with over 20 million experiences, attracting over 32 million daily active users. The best description would be the YouTube of Games, as the platform is populated largely with user-generated, multiplayer 3D worlds. Roblox has been around since 2006, but largely flew under the radar until recent years. In particular, the pandemic spiked its popularity as social gaming replaced meet-ups in person.

Anyone, anywhere can learn to use the free Roblox Studio engine and publish games to the platform. Because of this, there are vast amounts of content available; indeed, one of the Roblox core tenets for the metaverse is variety.

The quality of games on the platform ranges widely, but creating a hit game can bring community celebrity status among the massive community of 'builders'.

Roblox is downloaded once, and then the child can access new experiences by simply clicking play. There's no additional app to install or password, and the vast majority of games are free to play. As a result of this ease, kids play on average 20 different games every month. For this reason, hot games can quickly reach over 1 billion plays, with the top game 'Adopt Me' racking up that many *every month*.

Users customise an avatar to represent themselves in the virtual world. A large proportion of users change their avatar's clothing daily, connecting their real-life mood and identity (another one of the Roblox tenets of a metaverse) with their virtual persona.

Users, creators, and content are all connected by a thriving economy. Robux is the currency that flows through it, used to buy in-game items (power-ups and boosts), avatar customisation with gear and outfits, and – rarely – even entry to experiences. A 2020 study found that Robux are now the number-one thing kids buy with their allowance, above candy, magazines and even '*Fortnite*'. Top developers are able to make a living creating games for Roblox, and others bring in smaller but tidy profits.

With such an extensive mix of identity, content variety, frictionless entry to different experiences, and a thriving internal economy, why is Roblox not a true metaverse? Ben Thompson in Stratechery calls it, instead, a 'microverse' because "the traditional conception [of a metaverse] was a virtual world that rivaled the real world; anyone could plug into it from anywhere, with full interoperability. Roblox, though, is only Roblox."

Monetising the metaverse

A true metaverse isn't only a hang out; it's a marketplace where businesses can be formed and real money made.

In 2020, 1.25 million Roblox developers earned payouts totaling $329 million. Games are predominantly free to play, but many creators offer in-app purchases using Robux, bought online and added to players' Roblox accounts like pocket money. The Robux in one's wallet can be used for items or experiences across the platform.

Kids spend serious amounts ($1.9 billion in 2020) in Roblox, even though there's no tangible item they can take away from the platform. They invest in items for their avatar as self-expression and representation inside the world. They buy in-game upgrades for the same reason adults might buy better running shoes or a flashy car – seeking to advance to a next level, get a desired badge, or show off to friends.

In a fully-operational metaverse, digital items will have to persist across multiple, connected worlds. Goods bought in Roblox-world should also be available in Fortnite-world, Facebook-world, and so on, without having to repurchase them.

This means a metaverse must have secure purchasing, ownership, management and trade throughout its scope.

This is where blockchain, and more specifically Non-Fungible Tokens, come into play. NFTs use blockchain technology to record and track securely who owns a digital item. These can be anything from a trading card to a GIF, a work of art to a piece of music. 'Non-fungible' means that the unique item isn't interchangeable, contrasted with fungible tokens (like major cryptocurrencies Bitcoin and Ethereum) where each unit is interchangeable, one for one.

NFTs benefit both the creator and the end user. There's an immutable record of ownership and the transaction is completed securely via the blockchain, using a (fungible) cryptocurrency as payment. The creator benefits from the monetisation of their digital item (and most NFTs also have a future-sales commission built into the creator's contract).

NFTs are having a moment, perhaps a bubble, with a lot of money being spent on items with artificial scarcity. There's no reason why only ten versions of a digital picture can be created, as the marginal cost is near zero. When it comes to the economics of a metaverse, however, unique and verifiable NFTs are necessary to ownership verification and transfer.

Public service organisations will have to navigate the financial aspects of the metaverse, in order to make their presence within sustainable. Are services still 'non-commercial' if their monetisation is entirely internal – selling virtual objects or experiences to enhance audiences' connection and engagement with public brands? If external funding (whether from government, NGOs or underwriting) or licensing and merchandising are necessary, how will the public service content differentiate itself from other worlds to justify the different treatment?

Brands together

Most experts expect that the metaverse will envelop many stories, brands and characters. '*Fortnite*' is a prime example where licensing for 'skins' causes worlds (e.g., Marvel, DC, Premier League) to collide. Moreover, because a metaverse enables creation as well as consumption, companies' IP may show up in user-generated games or settings they didn't create (there are more than 1500 unofficial LEGO games in Roblox).

Companies will have to decide to what extent they're comfortable with sharing space and giving up some control to users. Dubit writes about managing a brand's 'fanatomy' through give and take with the audience. When people create art, fiction or other creative expressions around their favourite IP, the owner has to decide whether to allow, affirm or incorporate those ideas, or to shut them down. To the extent the brand encourages them, fans feel listened to and deepen their commitment to characters, stories or worlds.

In a metaverse, people will display their personalities and passions wherever they go – via their avatars, the games or spaces they create and decorate, the choices they make in where to spend their time. In today's mash-up society, it's likely that their expressions will cross and mix brands. As long as they're not doing so in a disrespectful, harmful or offensive way, it may be best to allow them latitude.

Will public service brands be comfortable sharing space with highly commercial brands, stories, characters and products? Given that for today's kids and youth "everything competes with everything", they already navigate across platforms without paying much attention to whether content is public, commercial or subscription.

How do the real world and the metaverse connect?

No matter how vibrant and expansive the virtual world, most of life happens in the actual world. So, while we will immerse ourselves in the metaverse, will the metaverse also immerse itself in us? What will we carry with us from cyberspace back into our day-to-day lives?

Some examples are easy to imagine: we may shop and buy inside the metaverse for goods to be delivered in physical form. Our avatars and resources from immersive space may get incorporated into our homes to keep us engaged and connected with the work, play or socialising we do virtually, or into our cars to facilitate autonomous controls.

Activities that occur in virtual reality within the metaverse can continue in the outside world via augmented reality. One of the earliest AR applications was Yelp's Monocle, through which the rating app overlaid reviews and recommendations into live street views through a smartphone. With AR, users can be accompanied everywhere by their metaverse avatars, resources and knowledge.

CHILDREN'S MEDIA FOUNDATION

Will there be television in the metaverse?

We've already seen that immersive worlds can draw huge participation in special events. Marshmello and Travis Scott concerts played concerts in '*Fortnite*', which also hosted the Fortnite Shortnite Film Festival. Roblox held an album release concert and Q&A with boy band Why Don't We. Minecraft's annual in-person Minecraft Festival migrated to the platform during the pandemic. Nate Nanzer, Fortnite's head of global partnerships, has said he can envision any of these platforms becoming a tour stop for bands.

Would we use the metaverse for our day-to-day TV/video viewing, though? If so, how would we navigate? As convenient as it might be, it's difficult to imagine a single 'box in the corner' TV viewing space where we'd go to screen across all companies, genres and content.

Metaverse TV could be organised and branded similarly to today's broad channels (e.g., Nickelodeon) with IP from a variety of sources. It could involve deeply branded spaces (e.g., an MCU 'world') where users might watch, play and interact with their favorite stories and characters from a single company.

The children's video environment has evolved into 'clubhouses' and 'portals.' In a clubhouse, kids affiliate with the umbrella brand (Nickelodeon or PBS Kids) as much as the specific content titles. Branding and packaging are integral to consumers' identification with the clubhouse, and fans look to connect with it beyond video and into games, merchandise and more.

A portal is simply a content gateway, like Netflix. There's little fandom for the brand, but there is usually substantial love for the IP within.

Will metaverse video venues be clubhouses or portals? For a number of reasons – scale and efficiency, multi-platform immersion, frequency of use, and more – the clubhouse model seems most likely.

Television may not look the same in the metaverse. Virtual, immersive worlds enable audience participation in interactive stories, creating the sense of truly being part of the action. '*Bandersnatch*' was Netflix' first foray into interactive media; since then, they've launched several interactive shows including a choose-your-adventure animated TV series based on '*Minecraft*'. Viewers input decisions that affect the course of the story, using their TV remote.

Moving closer to the gaming side of interactive media, '*Rival Peak*' launched in 2020 with a massive game-like reality show starring 12 AI characters – '*Big Brother*' meets '*Animal Crossing*'. In this quasi-reality show, the characters are contestants in a Survivor-type competition where the audience can influence the outcome by completing tasks and helping their favourite characters win.

For Generations Z and Alpha, just watching a TV show may seem mundane compared with socialising in Among Us, winning a Fortnite Battle Royale, or completing a Roblox 'obby'. Even when they're not playing a game, they're often watching someone else play, on Twitch or YouTube.

Conclusion: We're a long way from OASIS, but...

Barring a dystopian apocalypse like in *Ready Player One*, we're unlikely to get the OASIS anytime soon. We won't spend 20 hours a day in haptic suits and chairs, using the virtual world to avoid the real one.

126

We will, however, spend increasing amounts of time in virtual spaces, as we play games, engage with stories, concerts, shop, learn, socialise, communicate, and create. It may not all be fully immersive, but it will be deeply engaging. How should creators and regulators plan wisely now for a metaverse future, knowing that the space will morph and evolve substantially in the coming years?

For creators:

- The metaverse will be a great place to launch a brand. You are the 'gatekeeper' with no need to strike a distribution deal as you create and expand. Feedback from your fans will be fast and direct. However, it still will make sense to build your IP from a single point of engagement and then expand (albeit with a strategy for evaluating future opportunities).

- Leave space for your fans to shape your development. As described above, supporting art or fiction around your IP, listening to audience suggestions, and sharing behind-the-scenes glimpses of your creative work will encourage your followers to chase your stories and characters wherever you take them.

- Consider what your IP would look like as a fully-developed 'world'. If you were to create a space within a virtual 'mall':

    - Where would fans engage with your content?
    - How would you organise and navigate it?
    - How would you invite new visitors?
    - What is a new user's starting point?
    - How would you guide that user deeper into your space?
    - How would you grow new offerings over time?
    - What is the economic model?

- Think long term. If you build out a space in the 'mall' and don't maintain it, it will appear like an abandoned storefront, and kids will notice.

For regulators or governments:

- Develop now plans to ensure age-appropriate 'neighbourhoods' for children. If the metaverse proves too amorphous and global to regulate, then sign-post sites and experiences that meet 'safe-harbor' standards. As of March 2021, children's rights under the UN CRC are sustained in the digital world, including their rights to privacy, protection, education and play.

- Establish opportunities to populate the metaverse with public service content reflecting diverse national and global cultures, created by indigenous people.

- Support public service media or organisations building timely and important content such as news and factual for children, or otherwise engaging youth as active citizens, now and in their future.

- Work with the various 'owners' of the metaverse to establish fair access to public service content and experiences, whether via promotion or algorithm.

- Commercial providers should be encouraged to support the public service elements of the metaverse, whether through their own 'kitemarked' offerings or through in-kind or direct investing in public service content and creators.

For this generation of youth, "everything competes with everything". Video and games, digital and physical, blockbuster and niche, professional and UGC, learning and play, social and solo – young people move among their favourite IP, brands and stories based on their moods and needs in the moment.

The metaverse will make their choices and transitions more fluid and connected. Big studios already supplement their traditional brand-building in co-creation spaces like Roblox, facilitating organic content influenced by real-time interactions. Conversely, new storytellers are launching IP directly in the emerging metaverse. As creative tools become simpler and more accessible, we will see organic weaving together of microverses built around small but passionate fan-bases (the 1000 True Fans concept) and global franchise megaverses.

Young people's early adopter engagement needs to be taken seriously, now. The metaverse won't be a space for superficial marketing – kids see through and reject inauthenticity. Instead, it's where you'll meet your audience face-to-face and build worlds together. Are you metaverse-ready? ⊙

LIKE

JOHN DALE

A pioneering children's producer imagines a future-world where young people themselves have built a new, empowering and sustainable public service media for children across the globe.

This chapter was almost fully 'imagined' in a small hotel in Belgrade, Serbia, by six young people and a youth worker in late September 2007. Ana and Katia, two 13-year-old girls from the favelas in Rio de Jamaica were sat with Luka and Milos, 14-year-old boys from Borča, just outside Belgrade; and Jiera and Yash, Indian brother and sister born near Brick Lane, in East London. Marco, the 30-year-old youth worker and I had been leading a workshop all day, so we settled in the hotel's old velvet sofas, grateful for the rest, only to be gripped by an outpouring of random consciousness from these young people. Their imaginings had been triggered by a simple question in the workshop that day: What would kids' TV look like in 2035? This chapter tries to record that tumbling, disruptive concept as it poured out of them…with just a few contemporary updates from me.

LIKE 👍

It is 1st July 2035 and a special day, because exactly ten years ago a group of passionate kids TV activists officially launched *LIKE* (Life Influencing Kids Entertainment & Empowerment Ecosystem) that was to revolutionise global kids' storytelling. So, here was the Director General of UNESCO, no less, standing on the sunny steps of Children's Museum of Caracas in Venezuela, congratulating them on their success.

She reminded everyone of how *LIKE* had started in 2023, with kidfluencers Vlad and Niki, the Russian American brothers (152 million + followers averaging five billion monthly views on 16 channels and translated into 13 languages) joined forces with Diana, the then 9-year-old YouTuber broadcaster with 77 million followers and Ryan Kaji, the 9-year-old toys influencer with over 60 billion views. Like many of these technically illegal young publishers on the world's social media platforms, this group had become aware that their daily 'scream' at the camera was slowly losing the interest of their loyal followers. They were realising that they needed to 'bulk up' their content, but that required storytelling skills. The irony was not lost of them, as these talented social networkers had a reach of billions that traditional broadcasters could only dream of, but their content was thin and in danger of plunging them back into the obscurity of being 'normal' kids. Their slight panic at this dreadful thought was mediated by a Nigerian vlogger, called Oma Ikande. Like Malala Yousafzai, the Pakistani fighter for free education, and Greta Thunberg, the climate change activist before her, Oma was a naturally gifted 14-year-old communicator, but unlike those before, she was still searching for her mission. This young pioneer-in-waiting grabbed the moment and called together ten of these extraordinary young millionaire publishers on Telegram and *LIKE* was born. After their meeting, Oma's opening message to the world began:

> "I come from Africa, where the UN says 37% of all children on this planet will live by 2050; yes, you heard that right, that's 37% of ALL kids on this planet. In Nigeria, only 3% of our entire TV output has any original kids' programmes, and instead we're being fed with tired, old US cartoons presented to us as our national cultural diet. This makes me very angry. Today, I represent ten young global publishers under the age of 15. Currently, every single day, our group reaches 1.3 billion kids, and every day we are more determined to use this power to do something to change this. Today we say to all parents, politicians and broadcasters, now is the time to stop looking the other way."

The speech went viral with 137 billion views and amongst those who made contact with Oma were some powerful and informed representatives of kids' media, finance, education and tech companies from all over the world. Quiet messages of support – private sympathies and offers of help. A second meeting was convened and the young publishers, now known on the buzzing networks as 'The Ten' made a compact with twelve of these supporters, who immediately became known as 'The Elders'. They needed a name. Branding came naturally. These kids already had a common trust system with their audience, based on a simple:

LIKE 👍

In early 2024, the group published its intentions: *'LIKE (Life Influencing Kids Entertainment & Empowerment Ecosystem) will STIMULATE, working with the best independent kids' programme makers across the world; ACTIVATE all kids to feel empowered, so that they can tell their own stories; FACILITATE a highly collaborative ecosystem to support all members of LIKE to enjoy and learn from each other; and ENTRUST all our work to the care and open management of independent and experienced co-workers who will guide us."*

This SAFE Mission needed money. Clearly, The Ten had already amassed small fortunes themselves, but they needed 'grown up' patronage to make the bigger international institutions wake up. The first strike was a Middle East sovereign wealth fund, who were becoming terrified about the drain of their young people to Europe and the US, never to return. The fund managers had come to the conclusion that a decade of ignoring generations of kids had broken any bond their governments had with their own, younger generations and now the talent was departing, it was beginning to hit the bottom line as they moved from an oil-based economy to one more aligned with digital futures. A few hundred million was nothing to them to try and reopen that discourse with their kids. The Elders' initial concerns about content interference were quickly dispelled, as the financiers' motives were about regaining trust, not promoting traditional mantras. They were having to change too.

Perhaps the most radical innovation was that the whole viewing experience was set within a 3D synthetic gaming environment. When kids became members of *LIKE*, they adopted avatars. Members could not only watch in *LIKE*, they could explore, play and learn in *LIKE*. This is where the ACTIVATE part of the Mission became at least as important as the television viewing experience. *LIKE* assumes that you will do stuff, not just watch it. So, you can make and upload videos using the Story Tool and then see them reviewed in the 3D village cinema; you can test your fitness it in the virtual fitness centre; you can learn life skills, like developing emotional intelligence, through the games available in the *LIKE* School of Short Games. That's why the enterprise was not called a channel, or even a platform. *LIKE* was a 360° ecosystem living and breathing inside an awesome gaming world.

The first *LIKE 1.0* version was launched on 1st July 2025. It had 37 million followers and 5 million members, who paid the equivalent of $1 per month to access all the functionality. In other words, it was massively subsidised, as its initial programme budget was $90 million and The Ten and The Elders had appointed 32 people in 13 countries to manage the business and 39 youth workers to facilitate the *LIKE* Activate Hubs that ran skills workshops across their regions. Several more broadcasters had begun to support, with old archive that was modified; and the gaming industry did cross-promotion deals. The Ten had decided that there was no such thing as 'ethical advertising', as it was all annoying, so they had set an ambitious task of making the ecosystem inclusive, with no subscription charges. At the time of launch, many governments were struggling to pay for health and social care and ironically didn't see kids' television as relevant to that or a priority. In the UK, the BBC, pioneer of kids TV, was battling to prevent its own breakup, and it had become evident that their government's mantra of market forces coming to the rescue was in reality, laughable. However, certain wily politicians in the UK did recognise a far bigger issue coming down the line. The Covid-19 pandemic back in 2020/22 had brought into sharp focus the increasing gap between the digital literate and the digitally impoverished, left isolated in lockdown. This situation, left to the beloved market, would quickly and negatively hit the bottom line of UK Plc and *LIKE* offered the Government an opportunity to innovate. On 1st July 2026, exactly a year on from *LIKE*'s launch, the UK Government announced their 'Digital Life Scheme', along with yet another small extension to the Young Audiences Content Fund. On the registration of birth, all children will receive a voucher that they can exchange, on their third birthday, for a digital device called SEED (Secure Entertainment & Educational Device). On each birthday, every year thereafter, the device would automatically upgrade its system, to keep in step with application development. The step-change for the *LIKE* group was that in the UK this would be sold with the BBC and *LIKE* software already loaded at no cost.

During 2027, several governments followed suit and the SEED manufacturer became part of The *LIKE* Group organisation. All profits were channelled back into the three parts of the mission – Stimulate, Activate and Facilitate. Communities of interest grew strong within the ecosystem, and The Ten and The Elders made sure that these editorial communities were reflected in the commissioning of programming. Perhaps what was the most fertile aspect of this early stage was the influence the kids had on the programme makers. In the early digital era, even the most visionary producers of kids' programming viewed content created by kids as an innovative add-on. But as broadcast compliant technology was incorporated into quite ordinary mobile phones and three-year-olds mastered interactive menu systems on editing software quite easily, the notion of User Generated Programming began to feel patronising and out of step with what was really going on in the kids' preferred universe of the internet. From the outset, *LIKE* reversed this idea, bringing back control to the kids, who were turning from 'viewers' to 'doers'. The Ten commissioned some of the world's top software developers to create tools that enabled kids' ideas to become fully immersive video experiences on the SEED screen all over the world. They developed automatic language translation and audio dubbing that allowed players to understand and review other members work from anywhere in the world; templates for documentary production; guidance tools for collaborative drama production; and amazingly powerful animation tools that could transfer a five-year-old's imaginings into stunning cartoon experiences.

This had a profound effect on the programme makers. The Ten assured them that their traditional storytelling skills were never going to be replaced by kids' generated content, but that their role as STIMULATORS was to make their programming become a more 360° experience. These producers began to flourish in this more gamified and interactive holistic environment. Over time, this 360° approach created a highly immersive ecosystem of content that members could navigate around, following their own instincts and curiosity.

Technically the delivery of *LIKE* became a challenge. Despite generous donations from many software and data storage businesses all over the world, the membership still wanted a mix of delivery platforms to ensure inclusivity, and the storage need was becoming vast. By 2028, the sheer number of OTT streamed channels had lived up to its name and had become an Over-the-Top chaotic jungle of brands that were difficult to navigate. Meanwhile, the regularly predicted demise of linear channels was still not happening and, in fact, many adults were preferring the serendipity of an old-fashioned scheduled set of programmes, linked to the time of day. The giants like Disney+ and Netflix continued to dominate, but their initial 'gross' investment meant that continued growth into world domination was an economic necessity, and kids' services were not always that relevant to the bemouths' core financial needs. Meanwhile, the YouTubers kids' content continued to be under funded and poorly mediated. *LIKE* was poised for its next growth spurt.

In January 2029, *LIKE 2.0* launched its linear channel in 23 countries, alongside a massive rebuild of its web portal, gaming platform and online retail store. It's library now had over 9,700 hours of kids programming and it had developed 157 learning games, many of which were being delivered as download donations to some of the lower income regions' schools. Three more wealth funds in the US, Hong Kong and Norway had joined with a UK philanthropist to boost the fund that, combined with five government's kids' content funds, had grown to be a $1.3 billion future investment fund.

Not everything went smoothly. The talent pipeline required by the growing *LIKE* Group became an issue three years after launch. The Elders worked with the Open University and MIT to create an unusual two-year fast-track remote degree, as well as a set of 25 short courses all delivered, and capability-measured through an immersive gaming format. Meanwhile, localisation also became important. Kids in Mumbai naturally wanted different cultural reference points to those who lived in Leeds and Jakarta. *LIKE* redeveloped the Activate Hubs, adding additional teams of trained young media facilitators and care workers, which became known as *LIKE LABS*, that supported both the creativity and the health of their young producers. They also had small budgets to commission local professional producers and quickly the international schedule became populated by 20% of regional outputs, making the content STIMULATION even richer.

So, where were we? Oh yes, on a steps outside the Children's Museum of Caracas with UNESCO and the LIKE Group, facing the world's press. The Director General has come to Venezuela to announce a new joint investment into The LIKE Group by UNESCO and the WORLD BANK, as part of its 'Global Balance for Children' initiative, to sustain *LIKE*'s educational outreach programme and fund the new SEED device roll out across the world. She reminds her audience that *LIKE* has grown from a success story to a phenomenon and can now be classified as significant part of human history. Membership is at 470 million kids, aged between 3 and 16 years old. Over 120,000 independent professional companies from 37 countries now service the ecosystem, with the average employee number being 7 people, with an average age of 25. Content from members on the linear channel remains at 45% of output, every day. 57 universities host the *LIKE* degree courses around the world. The Ten still remain the same pioneers, whose average age is now 24 years old. There are 132 co-opted Elders from 25 countries managing the editorial commissions and localised outputs from the 12 *LIKE LABS*. The virtual management of LIKE is now coordinated from Leeds, The Hague, Dubai, Nairobi, Jakarta, and Mumbai.

"This is a truly remarkable story of our ability, when things hit rock bottom and our children were manifestly being forgotten, to turn things around."

The applause for the Director General dies as Oma, still the spokesperson for The Ten, walks to the microphone. As always, she is the one parents and kids around the world want to hear.

"Forgive me Director General, but that's not quite true. The Ten started this, but it was those initial five million of our members worldwide that 'turned

it around', not politicians, or broadcasters. In many ways, we were the
forgotten ones, consigned to bottom of the 'change agenda' by regional
wars that killed kids, rather than ending the greed or religious intolerance;
the pandemics that made child poverty and isolation unbearably worse;
and the collapse of economies, where governments worried more about
investors than families. And yet, new forces were surfacing that came from
within the people themselves – they just needed signs of believable hope to
gather around, as happened in climate change and racial intolerance. So, like
those movements before us, The Ten called out and kids answered.

"We don't just want TV, we want a space, a digital place where we can learn,
laugh and play safely. That means we want storytelling that makes us think;
entertainment that makes us smile; challenges that enables us to cross
borders and play together; knowledge that satisfies and then increases our
curiosity. We need something that is designed to be an adventure, that uses
all of our senses and reaches everyone, not just those who can afford smart
devices who live in rich countries."

Oma had the crowd spellbound now.

"People say that before, our increasingly small number of brilliant kids'
broadcasters were held back though lack of money. We have shown that
was not really the case. There are vast amounts of money in the world, but
they are just not being channelled into things that are necessarily needed
or run by people who can't be trusted. With the help of our amazing
Elders, we used our collective voice to raise just enough from investors
and broadcasters to get going, and then it was a matter of making sure
that the ecosystem delivered what was actually needed in a modern
digital ecosystem, allowing the numbers to naturally grow, making LIKE
sustainable. Thank you everyone for your support and belief in those early
years. I promise you, we will continue to listen more than talk, stimulate
more than self-satisfy, facilitate as much as manufacture, and care for all,
not just those who have choices. We have only just begun!"

The statistics related to the reach of the young social media publishers are all
verifiable for their current audiences in 2021. Oma Ikande is, however, fictional. This
vision emerged from six young people who were attending a storytelling workshop
organised by Eurokidnet, a charity set up in the Netherlands by a passionate advocate
of kid's media, Sannette Naeyé. She had enlisted the support of Anna Home OBE
on her board, and they had asked me to help them grow the organisation. The
mission was to recruit kids living in areas that suffered from acute poverty and where
children's voices were not being heard. We created a storytelling media tool kit for
kids and established youth workers in Rio de Janeiro, Belgrade, Budapest, and in the
East End of London's Pakistani community. Early software developers of automated
language translation donated their prototypes so that kids could review online each
other's short films and over two years, 37 of these were watched by thousands of kids
all over the world. This small experiment ended with a final Story Lab in Belgrade
and that's where, on that amazing night, six kids told me about their dream of kid's
TV. I hope it is a useful contribution to this very important debate.

ONCE UPON A TIME, THERE WAS A BROADCASTER... RESPONDING TO THE DISTRIBUTED RISK OF CHILDREN'S PROGRAMME PRODUCTION AND CONSUMPTION

DR KARL RAWSTRONE

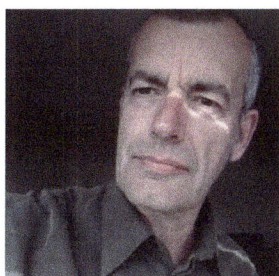

An examination of the consequences of the widening media landscape and what that means for the future of content creators and also the content consumers.

This contribution argues that the widening of the market for children's programmes has had two consequences in relation to risk. Firstly, organisational risk is distributed outwardly from broadcasters to individual producers. This is most-commonly framed in financial terms, but also includes the diffusion of institutional intelligence and the loss of advocacy traditionally housed in broadcasters. Secondly, the risk to consumers is distributed away from public-service broadcasters and the regulator to individual viewers and families as children's media consumption takes in an increasing proportion of unlicensed online content.

The broadcaster-facing regulatory model has failed to match pace with the economic, technological and cultural shifts in children's programme production and consumption. The distinction between traditional broadcast and online content production is not reflective of children's platform-agnostic viewing and the producers', rather than the broadcasters', visibility to the consumer is increasing.

With a reduced centre-of-gravity traditionally provided by the broadcaster, producers lack a self-regulation, advocacy, and support network. Given the mixed landscape of children's media consumption, such support should not be based upon platforms and technologies but upon the act of producing children's content.

The cultural constant of children's programme consumption

Children's programmes play a part in forming and reflecting our early lives. Readers of a certain age will remember television programmes that they grew up with and be able to recall the plots, characters, shared hilarity and fear, and excitement at sitting down to watch the latest episode of their favourite shows. 'That they grew up with' is a key phrase. Those stories, personalities and characters became part of our lives – household and playground names shared with families and friends. Television programmes brought the world to us and us to the world. We could, at the best of times, see ourselves reflected on screen and experience the unfamiliar. We not only learned about ethics and morality but also found respite from the mundane and worrisome.

The television schedule, and the physical television itself, were significant structuring elements of our lives. The adult schedule, for a short time in the late afternoon and early evening, gave way to our world. Parents, siblings and carers had the opportunity to either share in that world or retire to their own boring grown-up activities safe in the knowledge that we were in good company.

This, of course, is an idealised and nostalgic rendering of what some might refer to as a golden age of children's programmes. The reality for many was different, particularly given the middle-class white-British dominance of programme production, concentrated in a very few broadcasters' hands. Over four decades, however, the decentralisation of production, from in-house to independent production, the move of children's programmes onto their own channels, the addition of more broadcasters, and the growth in online content platforms has significantly expanded the range, availability, and aims of children's programmes. Critically, however, while the economics of production have changed almost beyond recognition, the cultural value of children's programming has not. Children's programmes retain their formative, structuring influence on children's lives and the need for children's media to embody public-service values, regardless of the mode of production or consumption, remains critical.

The disaggregation of children's programme production and consumption

In the 1950s there were two places where children's programme production and consumption were concentrated: at the BBC and the ITA studios (colloquially known as, and latterly becoming, ITV.) In 1985, the BBC branded its children's output as Children's BBC, shortened to CBBC, which launched as a discrete digital channel, alongside its sibling for pre-school viewers, CBeebies, in 2002. CITV, the children's offering from ITV, launched in 2006. In the intervening years, dedicated children's channels began broadcasting on satellite, cable and digital services (The Children's Channel in 1984; Nickelodeon and Cartoon Network in 1993; The Disney Channel in 1995; Pop in 2003,) several spinning-off sibling channels (for example, Cartoon Network launched Boomerang in 2000 and Toonami in 2002.) With all but the

BBC's content being funded by advertising revenue, there was a fragmentation of the total spend on children's programme production, so more-cheaply acquired content tended to dominate over original production on the commercial channels, while original content occupied a higher proportion of the BBC schedule.

The UK launches of Apple TV in 2007, Netflix in 2012, Amazon Prime Video in 2014 and Disney+ in 2020 provided consumers with additional sources of children's programmes and producers with additional commissioning opportunities for original content. In addition, the prevalence of on-demand platforms available on a number of digital devices – now the norm rather than the exception – means that the physical television set and the programme schedule have a decreasing grip on the structure of children's media lives.

Perhaps most disruptive to the children's programme landscape, and challenging the term 'programme' itself, is the entry into the market of browser-based social-media video-hosting platforms, including Facebook and Flickr in 2004; YouTube in 2005; Whatsapp in 2009; Instagram in 2010; Snapchat and Twitch in 2011; and TikTok in 2017. The relationship between platform provider, producer and funding in these cases ranges from a purely self-publishing (and ultimately pay-per-click) model, through to sponsorship and product-placement deals. From 2012, YouTube provided in-house production facilities and support for content-creators through YouTube Space. YouTube producers are often found via 'channels' and the platform launched a dedicated children's app, YouTube Kids, in 2015. Such are the contradictory divergences and convergences of the market for original children's content that the BBC is planning to move its in-house children's and education production teams into BBC Studios in order that they can compete for commissions from other broadcasters and platforms.

There are now more platforms and publisher-broadcasters of children's programmes than ever before. This provides far greater opportunities for the broadcast of original content and for a far greater diversity in that content. The structuring and curating influence of the physical television and the linear television schedule has been eroded. This provides greater viewer choice but also means that shared viewing experiences are far fewer. Both the production and consumption of children's content have been disaggregated to the point of individualism.

Independent production as a distributed risk network

What became known as the UK's independent television production sector was greatly stimulated by the formation of Channel 4 in 1982. Formerly restricted to working in-house for broadcasters or competing for the limited number of original content commissions, television producers now had available to them a whole channel dedicated to publishing independently produced original content. This market was further stimulated by The Broadcasting Act 1990, which introduced the independent production quotas, requiring public service licensed broadcasters to commission 25% of their content from independent producers. The Communications Act 2003 allowed independents to retain intellectual property rights in their content, with the consequence that broadcasters offered lower production budgets, distributing the risk of programme funding to the producer.

Through the 1980s and 90s, producers who had learned their trade on film productions and as broadcasters' employees set up shop as independent production companies and began competing for schedule space and budget. At the time, these independents were portrayed as an innovative and entrepreneurial vanguard. Through the 2000s, however, the high levels of risk experienced by small independents led to them merging and seeking to become acquired by larger organisations, creating what became known as 'super-indies'. Some super-indies had turnovers as large as smaller broadcasters. They were able to spread risk through portfolio diversification and had more revenue to fund programme development – a resource-intensive process which precedes approaching broadcaster commissioners with programme pitches which may or may not succeed. Such is the uncertainty and risk for the independent producer seeking commissions that this century has seen ever more independents seeking the security of partnership with larger companies, including international and domestic broadcaster studios.

The actual independence of independent producers carries a great deal of emotional import. Creative autonomy, the excitement of risk-taking on uncertain programme pitches, and the fleeting chance of making it big, hold a certain attraction. However, the realities of paying employees, supporting families and maintaining a professional identity as a producer are ever present in the mind of the independent producer. Independence is a trade-off between financial risk and creative autonomy. Many owned independent producers retain what they refer to as an independent culture – an organisational identity and way of approaching production which is distinct from their owning studio.

Independent producers are not independent, but rely on sets of negotiated dependencies. They are dependent on their production teams, on broadcaster clients, on policymakers, and on the shifting cultural trends of the viewing public. The producer is a hub at the centre of these dependencies, capable of creating the complex synergies required for programme creation, but also exposed to the risk of this complex web breaking down. The producer's role is concerned with forging and maintaining interpersonal and interorganisational relationships. It is ultimately a social role, and a lonely one.

In my research, talking to independent producers revealed the lonely risk-management that was at the centre of their role. They cherished their production teams, worried about the viability of their companies, and were frustrated at the challenges of getting original content commissioned. Those that had forged ownership deals with larger studios appreciated the support and security that this provided. Those that had maintained their true independence faced the day-to-day threat of career-ending failure.

What also was revealed was a desire for, but a remarkable lack of, collegiality and support among producers. Independent producers are, of course, in competition, and they are also competitive in nature. Whatever attempt the producers I had spoken to had made to create mutual support networks had failed. The overall picture was a rather solitary, risk-infused day-to-day existence leading teams on creative adventures.

Both this recognition and the fact that independent production companies find many ways of organising their existence and behaviours, referred to in academic literature as 'production cultures', means that portraying independent production as a sector, while facilitating the measurement of economic and cultural influence on a national and international scale, masks the individual and greatly diverse experiences of working in this way.

Many older independent producers learned their trade working for broadcasters or large independents, striking out alone when the time came for them to express greater creative autonomy and to experience a riskier, and potentially more profitable, environment. This currently happens less. There are more job opportunities for production workers in independent companies than within in-house broadcasters. This has two implications. Firstly, the vast institutional knowledge of the major public service broadcasters is no longer diffused through the wider trade. Secondly, the responsibility for learning on-the-job is distributed between the independents. Employees often work on short-term and freelance contracts, moving between companies to gain experience and making career-developing moves in doing so. Once centralised in public-service broadcasting, the underpinning principles of production and responsibility for learning them have become distributed across a wide and disparate network.

Self-publishing – the ultimate risk distribution network

As the Ofcom Children and Parents: Media Use and Attitudes report 2019 shows, scheduled terrestrial television holds ever decreasing attraction for young viewers. With the prevalence of smart-device ownership among younger consumers comes a greater engagement with social-media based publishing platforms, with YouTube preferred to both video-on-demand and scheduled television by 5-15 year olds.

Prevalent on these platforms are vloggers. These producers are often also presenters, forging seemingly one-to-one relationships with their viewers, who are potentially able to communicate directly with them, sometimes in real time. While some may have some media education, few if any have learned their craft in the employment of broadcasters and are self-taught. Viewing of regular online streamers and vloggers reveals that there are some elements of community between producers, who may 'name-check' or guest on each other's posts, and there may be an element of peer-assisted learning or learning through co-observation as producers strive to make more attractive content. Predominantly, however, the self-publishing producer's life, and professional risk, is even more individualised than that of the independent television producer.

With far lower overheads than traditional television production, however, this individualised risk-reward relationship makes good business sense for the most successful producers. Some producers have the support of sponsoring companies who may provide, as well as content to cover – such as commercial goods to promote – production equipment and some training. Producing, of course, is not only the physical creation of content, but the editorial oversight of its values. Rather than television production in the UK, which was founded on public service values, self-published online content was founded on principles of individual popularity. Clicks, likes and subscriptions provide the self-publishing producer with self-validation and revenue.

For the time being, and sometimes only tacitly, television production in the UK remains influenced by its public service foundations, online self-published content has no such history. This is not to say that the values demonstrated by a great deal of self-published content are incompatible with those of public service television, but those that are demonstrated are learned in an inferential fashion and are also influenced by a far greater range of cultural values. This is not necessarily a bad thing, as the diversification of content, within bounds, serves to widen the range of experiences available to consumers. What we understand in the UK to be public service values are, it would seem, obvious, but this is in fact the result of very specific culturalization over generations. Producers of children's programmes for television in the UK have both tacitly and explicitly learned how to adhere to the editorial guidelines and regulation of public service television.

Ofcom's regulation of online and traditional content continues the increasingly challenging task of ensuring the wellbeing of media consumers. There is, however, a great difference between defending child consumers from explicitly harmful material and promoting content which offers the very best of what children's television and its contemporary analogues can provide. Television retains, and online content promises, a vast developmental resource for children. The Ofcom Children and Parents: Media Use and Aattitudes report 2019 states, however, that fewer parents now than five years ago consider the benefits of children viewing online content to outweigh the risks. With the distribution of production, and its risks, being more widely distributed, so also is the responsibility for risk mitigation decentralised, sitting ultimately with, in the best case, the concerned parent or carer and, in the worst case, the child consumer.

Responding to distributed risk in children's programme production and consumption

This contribution does not aim to paint independently-produced or self-published children's content as inherently dangerous. Neither does it argue for a recentralisation of children's programme production, consumption and regulation. Four decades of television and media policy and global economics have ensured a wider and more open market in production than ever before. The genie is very definitely out of the bottle and will not be put back in. The contemporary context of the individualisation of risk for both producers and consumers comes with great opportunity, as well as challenges.

Over the space of four decades or more, children's programme production and consumption has moved from a coherent, culturally ring-fenced, trusted and safe space, where risk was centralised in a very few licensed broadcasters, to an open, disparate, and diverse space where risk has been distributed to individualised producers and consumers. Taking the landscape as a whole, producers no longer want to be told what to produce and child consumers do not want to be told what to watch.

So, how may we respond to this challenge and maximise this opportunity? Top-down regulation has limited impact on the fine details of content production and consumption, but it is in the fine details that excellent, memorable and beneficial content distinguishes itself from the rest. These fine details represent a search for excellence in production. A divided production base, however, cannot benefit from institutional learning, support, and advocacy and the wide distribution of content across platforms makes the very best content harder to find for consumers.

A response to these circumstances should include a shift in what is considered the independent production sector and how this is represented. The exclusion of online and social-media production and quasi-professional content-creators from the standard industrial classification of television production reflects neither the contemporary landscape of children's media production nor consumption. Removing the platform-based classification-gap between traditional and emergent production and consumption models would allow for a coherent approach to governing, guiding and supporting all creators of children's content, bringing television and online producers together, reflecting the mixed landscape of children's media consumption and infusing it with the values of public service.

This shift in perception makes it even more clear how disparate and disconnected children's producers actually are. Independent production across broadcast and online platforms demonstrates a far greater diversity in both organisational culture and content than was present 40 years ago, but producers are provided with far less institutional memory and support than was available to the traditional in-house producers. We need to consider, therefore, how to both maximise this diversity while also supporting independent producers' learning and support needs, in the interests of providing child consumers with excellent content and their families with greater trust in that content. Television producers and online producers have much to learn from one another, but the current broadcaster-focused and platform-specific policy models do not provide a forum for them to do so nor a platform from which to advocate their work.

What is at stake are the ethics and morality of children's programme production and a care for both the producers and consumers of this content. Just as the risks of production and consumption have been individualised and distributed, so must we distribute the support for and advocacy of those wanting to make the most of this unprecedented opportunity.

OUR CHILDREN'S FUTURE

ED VAIZEY

An insight into how our politicians might pull the levers of government to create a new public service media system that meets the needs of the children's audience.

There are always more urgent issues demanding the attention of ministers and MPs than there is the time in the day or the space on the legislative timetable that is needed, perhaps never more so than now. And in these times, it can be difficult to make an argument for the arts sector as a priority, when there are so many other businesses in need of support, as well as schools and hospitals. But even as we debate how best to cope with the immediate crisis, we must look to the future. What sort of world will we build as we emerge from this crisis? What is the future that, as parents, we imagine for our children? And how will our children develop the resilience and creativity that will allow them to make the most of that future?

When we think about how we can prepare our children, we turn first to our schools and our teachers. And rightly so. Our education system is at the heart of our community efforts to open young people's eyes to the complexities of the world they live in, whether that is the world of work, politics or even personal relationships. We ask our schools to teach and then uphold our shared values of fairness, tolerance, inclusivity and respect for our democratic institutions and the rule of law. With great dedication and professionalism, teachers take on that responsibility, guiding each generation to become informed, active citizens of the United Kingdom.

But increasingly, many of our children are getting one clear message from their teachers and parents and a very different, often confused message from the media content they access on their phones, tablets and laptops. Instead of engaging with content curated for them by a well-regulated public service broadcasting system, our children are increasingly watching content 'curated' for them by an algorithm. Instead of being guided toward diverse content that touches on different topics, ranging across genres and formats, they are being guided toward what they 'like'. To be precise, they are guided toward whatever the algorithm, and its analysis of data from millions of users, has calculated is most likely to entice that specific user to keep watching video content on that platform. And what is wrong with that?

Where exactly is the problem? We all want to watch stuff we like. Certainly, if you asked a child that question, they would answer loud and clear: "*I want to see more of what I like.*" However, as adults, we have – hopefully – learned there is a difference between what we want and what we need. We might want to watch another episode of the latest drama 'box set', but we choose to watch a news bulletin because we understand we need to hear what is happening in the world. We might like the idea of watching a favourite sitcom episode for the twentieth time, and sometimes we end up doing exactly that! But the next time, perhaps, we choose a new show on an unusual theme or about a place that we know nothing about. As adults, we understand that if you don't challenge yourself, or only watch what you've always watched, you risk simply reinforcing your beliefs and prejudices.

That's the danger of algorithmic interactions with media content. They can be limiting and, inadvertently, can restrict our freedom to choose. I stress 'can' because there are many benefits to the technologies we have developed that allow media companies to personalise digital experiences. But they work best when the user is savvy enough to make the algorithm work for them, instead of vice versa; when they are able to break away from some predetermined pattern of engagement. There are times when you have to resist where the algorithm takes you. And despite claims to the contrary, children and young people are not always that savvy around technology. It's true they learn fast, but their learning tends to be focused on breaking down barriers and getting around parental restrictions to access more of what they like, rather than developing discernment. The younger audience, in general, is not great when it comes to thinking about getting what they need.

At this point we are all probably thinking about some of the popular video sharing platforms (VSPs) and, in particular, the big players in that space, such as YouTube, TikTok and Facebook. Those platforms are extraordinary success stories. They demonstrate just how responsive businesses can be in a free market. They are smart, agile and completely focused on what their customers want, constantly analysing the data and adjusting systems to maximise value to those customers. The only problem with that is their customers are not the young people who access content on the platforms; their customers are the businesses that are selling the products and services advertised on the platforms. The children and young people who access the video content are actually the product that is being sold. The more users on the platform, the higher the price for placing an advert.

Does that sound terrible? Really, it's not. It's exactly the same business model you find in commercial television. ITV is in the same game and we are all fine with that. We, the audience, get to watch 'free' TV and ITV makes a profit from the ad sales. We all win. Although up until very recently, there was one important difference between ITV and YouTube, TikTok and Facebook. We come back again to that very dull but important concept: the regulatory framework.

ITV is a commercial public service broadcaster and part of our existing PSB system, along with the BBC, Channel Four and Five. It operates under the watchful eye of the communications regulator, Ofcom, and is subject to the legally-constituted

CHILDREN'S MEDIA FOUNDATION

Broadcasting Code, which attempts to set quality thresholds for programmes by, for example, laying down guidelines on impartiality and accuracy in news and current affairs. Ofcom regulations also offer protection to both contributors and audiences by setting down rules on fairness and by requiring broadcasters to take steps to avoid causing harm and offence.

As of October 2020, TikTok, along with some other smaller VSPs, is now regulated by Ofcom. It is a move in the right direction, although the details of how services will comply with the new regulations are still being worked out. As it stands, the VSPs are only required to take "*appropriate measures*" to protect children from potentially harmful content, in contrast to the stronger wording contained in the Ofcom Broadcasting Code, which lays down a guiding principle "*to ensure that people under 18 are protected*" and requires broadcasters to take "*all reasonable steps*" to protect people under 18. But, as I've said, this is a move in the right direction and the Government is committed to extending that regulation when it introduces the Online Harms Bill.

YouTube is another matter. Although YouTube, according to Ofcom's research, is the most popular media platform for UK children, it does not come under the new regulations for VSPs, because YouTube is based in Ireland, not in the UK. Irrespective of where a media company operates, it is regulated by the government of the country where its European business is registered. So, when there is a particular issue the UK would like to see addressed by regulation, the UK is dependent on the goodwill and judgement of the Irish government and EU directives. Of course, there is excellent cooperation between the two governments, and even if there wasn't total unanimity on the best way forward, what are the chances of a large, global media company seeking to exploit any difference in opinion? Heaven forfend.

But again, as things currently stand, the only regulation Ofcom has brought forward with respect to VSPs is directed towards preventing harm and controlling advertising. We have not even begun to consider the thorny question of how a new regulatory framework might try to work with these media platforms to change the *quality* of media experiences for our children.

The point I am making is that this is going to be hard. We are dealing with powerful companies that work across national jurisdictions and have their roots in a very different tech media business culture. In the United States, businesses are familiar with the concept of regulation designed to prevent harm, but far less comfortable with regulation requiring them to do good, which is a fundamental principle of the UK's public service broadcasting system. So, if we decide that what we have isn't working for our children, and that to help them grow and learn about the world we need to change our PSB model into a new public service media model, that will encompass those platforms beloved by the children's audience, then we will probably have to offer the YouTubes and TikToks of this world a large carrot while waving an even bigger stick.

But let's say that happens. Let's suppose we find there is strong public support for taking back control of the UK's media landscape, shaping it to our own needs and purposes. What will be on our shopping list? What exactly might we discuss with those platforms?

Setting aside the issue of harmful content – for which legislation is already planned and which the platforms are starting to address – here are a couple of things that these large and very profitable businesses could help us with. They could, for example, agree to divert a percentage of their production budget into making UK-originated, high-quality, public service media content, helping us to create safer, curated online spaces for our children.

The thing with online platforms is that you're either nowhere or you are King of the Castle, and when you become one of the dominant players, the profits are eye-watering. In Australia, Facebook, YouTube and Google – which owns YouTube – have steadily increased their combined share of the digital advertising market to 80%. The Australian government decided that enough is enough and is forcing Facebook to pay for using media content created by Australian businesses. The situation for YouTube and TikTok is different, because they do pay their content creators. But although some people make a lot of money from YouTube channels and TikTok accounts, most do not. The profits are not shared equitably and, because these platforms have dominant market positions, it's difficult to see how competitors will erode that profit margin. It's a cliché, but in the online world, coming second is nowhere at all and to the victor go all the considerable spoils.

YouTube and TikTok, Netflix and Disney, do make a significant contribution to our creative economy, with massive productions made here, as well as providing platforms for UK creatives. But this is not public service broadcasting per se, and nor is it necessarily culturally essential. So, perhaps it's time to consider a cultural levy, similar to the one that was recently proposed for Canada by their Heritage Minister, the Honourable Steven Guilbeault. It's a perfectly sensible approach. As Guilbeault puts it, it's about cultural sovereignty: we would be asking these companies to invest in particular forms of British content, perhaps children's media, in the same way that we require British commercial PSBs to make an investment.

That precedent harks back to the foundations of our current public service broadcasting system. When the government awarded broadcast licences to the original ITV companies, it was clear their dominant position as sole providers of television advertising was, in the words of the media magnate and owner of Scottish Television, Roy Thomson, "a licence to print money". In return for this business advantage, the ITV companies were required to divert some of their profits into public service programming. Today you could argue that Roy Thomson's licence to print money has passed into the hands of the media tech giants. Perhaps it is time they assumed similar responsibilities?

Finding the funding for public service media content for children is only half the battle. At the same time, we must consider how that content will be made available to the audience. And again, some of these companies could help with that, particularly YouTube and TikTok. YouTube, as previously noted, is the audience's 'go to' platform for video content with TikTok not far behind. Furthermore, YouTube and TikTok are free to access, which is an important prerequisite for PSM content. Isn't that an attractive scenario? The UK's number-one providers of videos for children helping to fund UK-originated PSM content that, to return to the refrain from my introduction, will help to open their eyes to the complexities of the world they live in, whether that is the world of work, politics or personal relationships, and will also help them to understand our shared culture and values; fairness, tolerance, inclusivity and respect for our democratic institutions and the rule of law.

But, I hear you ask, will they actually watch those videos? Is it just a waste of money, because children will still choose to watch their favourite influencers, celebrities, dance-craze videos, etc? That's hard to say. It depends on the quality of the content and how it is promoted to the audience. It has always been understood that if people are to engage with public service media content, it has to be properly publicised and promoted. And that is where we could, once again, turn to some of these companies for help in creating those positive media experiences for children. It goes back to the heart of how they operate: it goes back to the algorithm.

Words like 'algorithm' and 'data' have become tainted. They now sound sinister and representative of everything that is scary about the online experience. But very few things are 'bad' in and of themselves, and algorithms are whatever one chooses to make them. For obvious reasons, social media platforms and VSPs choose to create algorithms that keep people engaged with their content. In the early stage of a company, it's about attracting as many users as you can to build the buzz around the platform. For established services, it's about making sure you don't lose your user to some up and coming rival. The algorithm makes sure all its users get plenty of 'sugar'. And just like in food and drinks, media 'sugar' is good for sales, but not always good for your health. (In a wonderful touch of serendipity, Zuckerberg actually means 'sugar mountain', which seems quite apt.)

Could it all be different? Could an algorithm be created that would have less 'sugar'? Perhaps a public service media algorithm could help our children to experience a different perspective on the world. Such a new approach should never be dictated by government, but would involve guidelines worked out in discussions with the platforms, along similar lines to the discussions currently taking place with the food industry around actual sugar intake. Any agreement would have to apply to all platforms to prevent unfair competition, perhaps with a 'health' kitemark to help parents identify compliant services.

Many of the ideas I have discussed in this article are quite revolutionary. As a Conservative, you might think I would be uncomfortable with that. But throughout our history, from the industrial revolution to the welfare revolution that started after World War One, conservatives have embraced change when they could see it would be for the benefit of the whole nation. We now find ourselves in a position where radical changes to the regulatory framework for our media services has become essential. The pace of technological change that led to the growth of the tech giants and the streaming services means we now have to respond, and respond fast. Over the next year to eighteen months, we will be discussing what must go and what we will put in its place.

Even if you disagree with my suggestions for change, I hope I have at least convinced you that children and young people should be at the centre of this debate on the future of public service media and that their needs should be an absolute priority for government. We know lessons start at school and continue beyond school, and we know media experiences are pivotal in the development of children's attitudes and their engagement with society. Those experiences help them imagine their future, based on their understanding of our shared culture and their perception of their place in the community. And the truth is, we know that if we ignore their needs, eventually we will pay a price. ◔

A VIRTUOUS CIRCLE: CREATING A NEW ADDITIONAL FUNDING MODEL

TOM VAN WAVEREN

A respected and highly successful animation producer considers how we can create a funding system for 'local' content that is sustainable and affordable, without simply relying on additional public funds.

I have been working in children's television for 25 years and have had the privilege of working with producers and content from all over the world. In the past few years, I have learned a lot about diversity and representation, I have learned about what drives public service broadcast platforms, as well as commercial broadcast platforms, and I understand their different funding models and reasons for being. So, when asked to consider what the future of public service media should look like, I felt compelled to get engaged in the conversation.

My journey in understanding the importance of PSM started when I was told that what distinguishes humans from other primates is that we bury our dead and that we tell each other stories for education and entertainment purposes. We understand the world through the stories we are told as children and it is our ability to understand the constructs at the heart of these stories that allows humanity to organize the world. Stories allow us to debate with each other about our past, present and future.

These stories started around campfires or filling time while hunting and gathering. They were told at fairs and in castle halls and were later put down in books. They were taught in schools from when we settled down in agricultural societies all the way through industrialisation and urbanisation. And then finally they ended up on screens, which is where the importance of PSM appears in the picture.

Because, at that last step, something interesting happens; a lot of what has previously been left to the imagination is suddenly filled in and visualized. Instead of the story we are being told forming a visual construct in our mind, we are shown what we are supposed to imagine, where the story takes place and who is in it.

Imagine being an Asian girl being told the fairy tale of sleeping beauty. You can imagine yourself as the princess, the fairies good and evil, as well as the prince on his horse and the kiss, all of them can look like you and your world and you feel connected. Now imagine that same girl watching Walt Disney's 'Sleeping Beauty' set in medieval Europe and the experience suddenly becomes very different. You have moved your story experience to the screen and you are no longer in control of the imagining and no longer a candidate for the lead role.

My point is that children get the most out of stories when they can relate them to their everyday life. It helps them develop their sense of self, and that means that someone should offer them a healthy dose of such content, as well as making sure that everyone sees themselves on screen, irrespective of who they are or what they look like. And when I say 'get the most out of', I really mean that children need to see themselves on screen for validation, to gain confidence about their role in the world and to get to understand that world and options for their future within it.

One project that really helped me evolve my perspective in this regard is the series 'Pablo', which was first produced by Paper Owl Films for CBBC and premiered in 2017. CAKE came in to help finance and distribute to the world:

> "Five-and-a-half-year-old Pablo uses his magic crayons to turn his life passions and challenges into fantastic adventures and his feelings into colourful characters with a voice in order to face the real world with confidence. Pablo is on the autism spectrum."

For this series, all the scripts were written by writers who are on the autism spectrum, many of them first-time writers, and all the voices were provided by voice actors who are on the autism spectrum, again many of them doing this for the first time, leading to completely unique and wonderful stories.

Not only did 'Pablo' do really well on CBeebies, the series was successfully sold and shown internationally. However, my learning came from the many letters that the BBC received, and shared with us, from viewers in all age categories who are on the autism spectrum or have a loved one on the autism spectrum. They explained how seeing a series with a main character on the autism spectrum, for the first time in their lives, made them feel that they existed in the eyes of the world and were not outside of the world but part of it! What I learned from this experience is that representation goes much further than tone of skin or geographic setting. It goes to all core characteristics that define us as individuals. We need validation that others see us; it confirms to us that we matter to others and that we exist. It is important to realise that this is true for every child. Seeing children like yourself on screen, children who sound like you and live and operate in a world like yours. It is all part of that validation and an important condition for raising confident and resilient citizens of the world.

I had the same learning from my discussions with Malenga Mulendema, creator of 'Mama K's Team 4', currently being produced by Triggerfish and CAKE as a Netflix original, on which I am serving as Executive Producer. In 'Mama K's Team 4', four Zambian teenage girls fight evil in Lusaka, their nation's capital. It is a classic superhero series in most respects, but what makes it unique is that the series is based in Zambia; the four main characters are girls; and the whole cast is Zambian and Black. However, and this is what makes the series even more special, the visual style is inspired from the real Zambia and mostly created by African artists. The architecture is Zambian, the vegetation and lighting is Zambian, the food and the daily life in the street is Zambian. As Malenga explained to us, it is important that when Zambian and African children watch 'Mama K's Team 4' they realise that this series was made for them, as it is about their world as it really is. It is not made by people pretending for this to be Zambia; it really is. If you are an African girl, you will have many challenges ahead of you. 'Mama K's Team 4' will show these girls that they are part of the world, that they matter and that they can be heroes. There is no message that could be more important.

So how, you may ask, does this relate to the debate about the need for public service broadcast and the growing strength of streaming platforms and on demand viewing?

With the strong rise of North American media groups offering their content services to a growing global audience, it becomes interesting to consider if consumers are likely to get enough diverse and representative content offered on such platforms. This is particularly true when it comes to children.

All of these mammoth commercial corporations, be they Disney, Netflix, Warner, Apple, Amazon or others, have a strong focus on children's content, while their editorial approach is mostly global. They look for what works globally over what is relevant locally, with just a sprinkling of local in the mix. And if the content on these platforms represents a cultural point of view it's firstly North American, and after that it's a rich mix of content from all over the world.

And yes, these digital global content platforms do also commission content from UK independent producers and license-in already existing UK content, but what they are not focused on offering is a programming mix that relates one on one with each sub-demographic of children in the UK. These global digital players will entertain the UK children's audience without offering the resonance that well-targeted, culture-bearing and representative content does. Public service broadcasters, on the other hand, have a long tradition of providing that local representation and are consequently the most obvious candidates to keep providing it.

Which leaves the question of how children's content on public service broadcast gets funded and what can be done to secure enough funding going forward.

Commercial terrestrial broadcasters like ITV argued their way out of their obligations to offer children's programming in their schedules many years ago. Children's specialty cable channels have little or no obligations to invest in UK content, and the budgets of public broadcasters like the BBC have been diminishing with regular intervals over the last 20 years. As a result it has become increasingly challenging for UK producers to get their children's and youth content financed.

In the case of animation, which I know best since that is my background, Children's BBC today might offer 21% of the required funding for a project, leaving a rather humongous gap to be filled. Some of that can be found by producing in the UK or elsewhere and taking advantage of local tax credit, taking you to closer to the 50% mark of your required funding. The rest would need to come from foreign partners or investment, and they will be most interested when the project is not too specifically local, so it resonates with children in other territories to a sufficient degree. If forced to give in to such requirements, the producer effectively has to change the nature and purpose of the project in order to get it made.

Over the last few years, the Young Audiences Content Fund has played an important part in providing a solution in such cases, particularly for projects that have a strong UK and representative nature, but can there be other ways in which we make it easier for UK children's content to be funded and produced?

For such a funding system to be sustainable and affordable, it can't simply rely on asking for an increase in public funds. Instead, it should get all parties that offer content to the market, public or private, to share its revenues in a more equitable way with those who produce such content. It should keep those funds in the industry and allow the content producers to create more of the same going forward while providing a significant proportion of the funding themselves.

Concretely, all content platforms in such a system, theatrical, linear or streaming, would pay a usage fee into a content fund. The fees would go to an account in the name of the independent producer of the content for all UK-produced content shown by the platform. So, cinemas pay a contribution per ticket sold and broadcasters pay a contribution per programme scheduled or viewed on their platform, and that money goes into the content fund. A well-performing low-to mid-budget series or feature should make between one-third and a half of its costs back through this funding.

In the UK, the most logical manager of such a fund would probably be the BFI. However, the money would not be given to the BFI itself but would be held on account for the independent producer having produced the content. They can only use it to match funds from a platform – pound for pound – in their next project(s). Furthermore, it would be automatic and not subject to gatekeepers. In the start-up phase and for first time applicants, each project would be judged on UK specific parameters before committing to allocate producer funds in such cases. Money in the producer accounts of the content fund would need to be re-allocated to a new project within a few years' time, after which the funds get re-allocated to first-time producers.

As soon as it would be up and running, this content fund should mean that the independent producer would be financed more easily and would no longer be out-spent by a platform/broadcaster. Typically, and depending on genre, a commissioning entity would offer 20 to 30% to the independent producer for its project, the producer could match with 20 to 30% and tax credits and other funds would get a project fully funded or a long way there. The independent producer would consequently maintain a much stronger creative and business voice/position in the project and the system would guarantee keeping substantially more funds and profits generated by UK content in the UK.

Furthermore, it should also be written into law that any platform or distributor, local or foreign, would have to commit to a minimum percentage of their programming offered to the UK public being of UK origin. Some of that content would consist of original commissions from independent producers and some could be licensed-in existing titles. And naturally, there would need to be an obligation to pay into the content fund as described above for all the UK content on offer on said platform or distributor. This way independent producers get a whole new stream of funding to make it possible to fund and maintain UK content for children of all ages.

Across continental Europe, similar legislation is being put in place to protect local content and audiovisual industries, with percentages of local content requirements reaching up to 60% and where newly commissioned content needs to get commissioned from independent producers for 85% of that 60%. This avoids media groups setting up local production subsidiaries and benefitting from these funding structures directly themselves. And finally, a certain percentage of the local content should be defined as Young Audience Content Fund (YACF) approved/developed as well.

For the avoidance of doubt, my suggestion is that this system would not replace license fees; it would come on top of such fees and would be separate from development and production funds such as the YACF and Tax Credits. In the medium term, the need for a YACF would diminish and producer contributions from the content fund would replace its production investments.

There would be conditions on the use of funds from the content fund, such as a requirement to spend at least 80% of the part of the budget funded from UK sources within the UK. There would also be requirements to use a majority of UK lead talent and for the production to qualify as UK content under the BFI's criteria.

A final advantage of this system would be that it would reward producers for producing content that gets viewed and it would make independent producers more independent, as they would have legislation and financial resources to strengthen their position in the industry. It is a circular model where large amounts of money stay inside the system rather than being paid out to shareholders. This regenerative model would support the development of a truly diverse UK media landscape, with opportunity for new talent and established talent alike to access funding for local, representative content.

In today's world, where many of our campfires have turned into shared screen experiences, we can use this new approach to make room for storytelling that is reflective of the rich and diverse story worlds that make up the UK today. Simply by giving UK talent the microphone, we will enable them to continue to tell their stories to the UK audience and share them with the world. ◑

WHAT NOW? WHAT NEXT? WHAT IF...?

GREG CHILDS

Drawing together the themes contained in this report, the director of the Children's Media Foundation sets out the challenges we face and shares some ideas to inspire new solutions.

Having spent the last ten years as Director of The Children's Media Conference, considering the issues and potential for kids' and youth media in the UK, public service content for young people has been on my mind for much of that time.

For that reason I was thrilled when the Children's Media Foundation Executive Group proposed the Our Children's Future: Does Public Service Media Matter? project. The report has been informed not only by the contributions of an eclectic mix of essayists, but also by the many conversations with external experts and countless internal debates at CMF. My article is an attempt to pick up some of the ideas discussed, and to propose some possible futures for further investigation. Hence the title: "What now? What next? What if?"

What now?

The current situation in the UK is that public service content is delivered for children and young people primarily by the BBC – on scheduled television, online, and through the BBC's iPlayer, with the content funded by the Television licence fee. Complementary services come from the three commercial public service broadcasters, ITV, Channel 5 and Channel 4 in return for broadcasting privileges which are now, for the most part, irrelevant – the last outstanding one being prominence on the EPG. In Wales, S4C delivers a Welsh language service using designated funding from the licence fee.

De-regulation in 2003 meant that there was no longer a requirement for the three commercial public service broadcasters to commission children's or youth content, which led to them abandoning the younger audience. With little investment, other than from the BBC, Ofcom has, since 2007, consistently warned that there is failure in the children's marketplace in its Public Service Television Reports. Recently, Ofcom was granted powers to once again require the PSBs to carry children's content – on dedicated services such as CITV or E4 if appropriate. At about the same time and after much lobbying by CMF and others, a new Government initiative created a pilot fund for 'contestable content' dedicated to the Children's and Youth Audience, the Young Audiences Content Fund (YACF). Its three-year remit was to disburse £57m towards development and production projects. Invoking its new powers, Ofcom elicited commitments from all three commercial broadcasters to carry more children's and youth content, creating the appropriate conditions for take-up of projects part financed by the YACF, leading to, in the last couple of years, a resurgence of new content on CITV channel, Milkshake! and E4.

But as this revival takes hold, once again it is Ofcom's research that reveals the big issue now: the flight of the younger audience from linear public service providers to on-demand platforms, user-generated and shared content platforms, notably Netflix and YouTube.

How has this failure to retain the audience happened? Two missed opportunities spring to mind. In 2009 the planned on-demand service Kangaroo - a joint venture of the BBC, ITV and Channel 4 – was killed by the Competition Commission in a misguided attempt to keep the market favourable to nascent service providers. To quote the Guardian at the time: "This is a severe case of analogue thinking in supposedly digital Britain." In 2011, to address the problem of market-failure in public service in the UK, the CMF actually proposed a VOD service aimed at children, funded by a mix of Government and Lottery funding, with sufficient budgets to commission content and maintain a platform to deliver it. This might have held onto that migrating children's and youth audience, had it been available early enough to establish itself. It was ignored. A government without the foresight to save Kanga, was really not going to be that interested in Roo.

What happened more recently is even more concerning. In 2017 BBC Children's announced major additional spending – £34 million – some for the older children's audience, and some for the roll-out of what was essentially a kids' iPlayer. There was talk of personalisation, an iPlayer that would "grow up with you": an attempt to address some of those fundamental preferences young people are showing in their media choices. It did not materialise.

We are now in a landscape in which the traditional method of providing public service content is under threat from audience migration to platforms which are not necessarily safe for children and increasingly light touch regulation – both online and in television. The YACF is having an effect, but the commercial broadcasters are not keen to put in much funding of their own; and the BBC is under increasing scrutiny from Government and constantly facing cuts, which impact the children's and youth audience as much as any other.

What next?

Looking at the medium term, the threats to public service content for young people are fairly clear.

At the BBC, the Government has the licence fee in its sights. Like a dog worrying a bone, it skirmishes with it, backs off and then regroups and attacks again. Forcing the corporation to take responsibility for over-75's free licences was the first crisis. Followed by the threat to decriminalise non-payment of the licence fee. Both of these options would reduce the BBC's operating revenue. Longer term, there has been renewed talk of converting the licence fee to a subscription-based system. This would propel the BBC into direct competition for loyalty with Disney+, Netflix and many others. In the opinion of the Children's Media Foundation, subscription would ride a coach and horses though the eclectic, non-partisan, curated nature of public service content. The CMF is all for audience choice, but also cultural and societal good, and that requires a secure income stream that is responsive to the audience but not immediately beholden to its whims. The threat to the BBC in its current form, will colour the medium-term landscape as far as children, young people and public service content are concerned. And of course, the flight of this audience to other forms of viewing will potentially increase BBC weakness in the face of the financial onslaught.

There is little doubt that the Young Audiences Content Fund is – for the Government – another front in the covert war on the BBC. While the CMF supports it absolutely as a fantastic method of getting more funds into children's production in the UK, the recent budget cut, wiping 25% off its value, suggests that the Government intends to stick to the original timetable for closing the pilot in 2022. Why? Because 2022 coincides with the mid-term examination of the Television licence fee. It was always the stated intention to roll examination of the effectiveness of the Fund into discussions about the licence fee: if the Fund is to continue then it will be financed by top-slicing the licence fee and the BBC will have to give some of its funding to the YACF. At DCMS this is considered logical as, ostensibly, that is where the money came from in the first place. At CMF it is considered a disaster as the inevitable result will filter down as cuts to the children's budget at the BBC. It would be "robbing Peter to pay Paul". The YACF was meant to address the lack of budget at the public service broadcasters in light of reduced ad-revenue, etc. This money needs to be replaced not by the BBC, but by market intervention.

CMF will be lobbying hard for YACF to continue with funding provided through innovative new approaches: Lottery funding or levies for example. Lottery money is not impossible: the Cultural Fund finances film through the BFI (coincidentally the parent organisation of the YACF). This provision was not in the original scope of the Lottery Cultural Fund. It was added as a result of lobbying. Funding children's content in a similar way would be a popular decision amongst the public. Levies are already being applied in France and could, at their simplest, be a tax on advertising and subscription revenues at the on-demand providers. Levies or their equivalent get support elsewhere in this report, notably from Lord Vaizey and, in more innovative ways, from Tom Van Waveren in his contribution.

The CMF itself was born on the back of a levy. In the 1950s, a small levy on every cinema ticket, helped revive the British film industry in the face of massive post-war US competition. The Eady Levy was hugely successful, leading to a new wave of UK cinema and to the creation of our original organisation, the Children's Film Foundation, which funded over 140 kids' feature films. We are proof that levies can work!

The process of reviewing the licence fee is already under way and will conclude in April 2022. The Government has gathered a panel of the great and good in broadcasting to advise them on the future of the licence fee, with this remit:

> The PSB Advisory Panel will advise ministers on whether public service broadcasting remains relevant and what a modern PSB system should contribute to economic, cultural and democratic life across the UK. It will explore if current funding and governance models are fit for purpose.
>
> The panel will also support the government in considering the issues raised and recommendations resulting from Ofcom's ongoing PSB Review.
>
> Panellists will be expected to look at the impact of technology on audience habits and expectations as well as the financial sustainability of broadcasters and the overall structure of the TV market. This will include things such as video streaming.

One of the members of the panel, Lord Grade, said: "*Our public service broadcasting remit has served the nation well for over 80 years, but the time has come to review its relevance for the digital age and maybe redefine it.*"

In this 'digital age' then, it is disturbing that the Ofcom review mentioned in the remit hardly mentions young people, and not a single member of this advisory panel has anything other than marginal experience of the children's audience

And yet all the commentators, and so many of the articles in the CMF report, are clear that children and teens lead the way when it comes to the take-up of digital services and perhaps, more importantly, when it comes to evidencing new habits and practices: demanding immediacy of access, ubiquity across platforms, the potential to interact and participate, and the space to make as well as watch.

Not only are the younger audience not being served by this Government process, but the process itself is flawed if the young are not understood as the driving force of change. Having read David Kleeman's excellent article about the 'metaverse', and how public service content might work in that scenario, I wonder whether the great, good and old on the DCMS advisory group can even hope to understand the changes that lie ahead.

We already have a generation of children for whom the habit of watching the BBC stops at age five or six. This is precisely the situation faced by PBS in the USA, initially due to the success of the commercial channels, and now fuelled by all the additional competition online. In fact, some of those traditional channels – notably Disney – have morphed into on-demand services and more will follow. For a long time, the US public service provider has lost its viewers at 5 and regained them at 55. Not a recipe for public approbation and support. As Anne Longfield says in her excellent article: "If you want to engage kids, you have to go where they are."

And that's online.

Delivering content (public service or otherwise) intended for children online raises concerns about the use of algorithms for search and recommendation. The problem of proximity of content is still an issue even with YouTube Kids' app. The US Congress has recently queried the reasoning for the autoplay function (screening another video as soon as one ends) being "always on" in the app, and the possibility of unsuitable content finding its way onto a child's stream of viewing. The failure of the children's iPlayer was no doubt connected with data collection and profiling. Online safety is then part of the "what next?" equation.

In the medium term, we could well see significant changes in the governance and regulation of web platforms – and as a result, in their design. Already VOD operations and user-generated VOD (such as YouTube) come under a European regulatory regime and UK regulations fall into line with that. It's light touch and not far removed from 'self-regulation' but the precedents have been set.

Meanwhile the UK Government has tabled the Online Safety Bill with a clear intention of setting standards for websites, particularly in their dealings with children. The envisaged regulation is fairly toothless, but the principle of standards of the real world applying online is a start.

The Children's Media Foundation backs calls by 5Rights and others for child-friendly design by default. The next few years will see various battles over how this might be implemented – in the USA, the UK and Europe, but I believe change will come, partly because the Wild West nature of the internet has started to affect politicians and the political process. It means the giants' days are numbered.

So, looking at the next few years and asking "what next?" I think we will see more content delivery online, with further attempts to make that delivery safe. We will see further attacks on the BBC's source of funding, we may see Channel 4 privatised. We may or may not see the Young Audiences Content Fund revived – I fear with licence fee money attached. And we might see the public service broadcasters relieved of their obligations to serve the younger audience as they move away from PSB status.

Which begs the question of how the YACF will function in the future if the PSBs are no longer the ultimate recipients of its largesse…

And that brings us to Act 3.

What if?

In this section I would like to float some ideas that are not fully-formed but I think worthy of discussion. They deal with possible futures for delivering public service content to young people.

For any of these plans to succeed they need to address:

1. The purpose of public service content – particularly in relation to the young and their special needs. This includes its universality, and consideration of what genres and even forms of content it should include.

2.   How public service media should be funded.
3.   Who creates it.
4.   How it might be delivered.
5.   How it should be regulated.

Definitions of public service and its meaning for the young have been considered in several ways in this report. For my part, public service media should serve up relevant, age-appropriate stories – fictional and factual – that help people understand their world and the wider world around them. It should equip young people to assess what is true and to understand how they might be deceived; it should ensure that young voices are heard; reflect diversity of thought, culture and humanity; should challenge and stretch, surprise and intrigue the audience; offer variety, range and choice. It should entertain with underlying purpose and should inform in an entertaining way and above all engage its audience.

But it doesn't have to be delivered in a linear fashion. What might public service games look, or indeed feel like? I don't mean a few ancillary add-ons to the CBeebies website, but might there be a public service 'quarter' in the metaverse?

And for that matter, as social connection is now frequently an important aspect of gaming, what might public social media be? This doesn't necessarily mean "what does the BBC do in Facebook?" but rather, "what if Facebook or TikTok were the BBC?"

I have been known to ask what a public service fridge might look like. In all seriousness, we are moving into a future in which the Internet of Things and AI seamlessly envelop our lives, feeding on data to learn and providing ever more personalised service. Should this be a purely commercial activity, or through combinations of regulation and funding, are there public service alternatives? Will anyone on the DCMS Advisory Panel on the future of public service media ask about public service white goods?

With young people, collection of data is the sticking point. The current system of safety online is built around the flawed U.S. COPPA Regulations, which do not allow data harvesting from children under 13 without the consent of parents. But children are using YouTube, TikTok and others, either by falsifying their age or by accessing content without being logged in. Has the time come to consider some form of regulated data capture from children so that they can benefit from what AI, if used responsibly (or more to the point, if used with a public service purpose) has to offer?

Jeremy Wright, Secretary of State at DCMS from 2018-19, at a recent event which explored the concept of online 'good', (not the usual online 'harm'), when considering young people, asked whether we should reconsider the approach to collecting data from children. If AI cannot learn from children, then how can it serve children well by mirroring what a child is concerned about or interested in, how a child feels and what a child knows and needs to know at various life-stages?

If the BBC's iPlayer for kids hit the buffers over data collection, that is surely evidence that it's time for a rethink. This becomes particularly relevant if we move into a future in which the discovery of public service content might no longer be associated with a channel brand, or even a dedicated player for on-demand, but could be encapsulated in an algorithm.

What if… we opened up the number of public service providers rather than narrowing it down to the BBC?

What if…. anyone could apply for public funding to create content, provided they committed to adhere to certain public service principles, potentially arbitrated or curated by a body not unlike the YACF, or a publisher version of the BBC?

As an aside, what if the finance for that public service fund came from a mixture of a modernised version of the licence fee, based on a simple tax on households, advertising and subscription levies, Lottery funding and Government funding for public communication and education?

What if… that content could then be sold at subsidised prices, given it had been part funded by the public service system, to any channel or platform that might want it as part of their content mix?

What if… a public service algorithm existed – potentially operated, maintained and adjusted by the BBC – which instead of pushing advertising or more of the same or similar content, as the recommendation systems do now, it used a subtler method of creating some serendipity, assessing the value of the recommended content, prioritising content which had been tagged as public service and so on?

What if… that algorithm was made available to all platforms and content providers, on the understanding that they offer it as a service to their subscribers or users who wished to take the public service route through their media choices? At this point it becomes particularly interesting and relevant to the children's market, where parents might want to ensure their children received a more varied diet than they might otherwise experience.

Taking it a step further, what if Ofcom replaced the concept of prominence on the EPG with a mandatory requirement that all operators take the public service algorithm and make it available by choice to their users?

I recently discussed the idea of a public service algorithm with Mark Little, a former executive at Twitter, currently sitting on the advisory group for the future of Irish public service media. Some of these ideas grew out of that conversation. To quote Mark directly:

> "The public service algorithm (PSA) would – in tech terms – be a contextual recommendation system rather than a behavioural one. It would recommend the next piece of content based on the topics appearing in the first piece of content. In a perfect world, the system would show the young person a list of the words, topics and people in the piece of content they searched for and ask them to choose the keyword they want more of. So, it could plot a journey of understanding for the young person based on their intentional interest rather than stalking their browsing history.

> I think the concept of a public service algorithm would work best where the content experience is owned and operated by the public service content providers. But it could have applications where a platform like Netflix is obliged by prominence rules to include a public service media option – then the PSA would be a collaborative venture.

The final option is a high-quality public media content source which could be syndicated on to websites. This could be a good version of the very bad business model at the heart of content recommendation engines like Taboola, which offers all the spurious random click-bait stories that clutter so many news sites."

My final "what if…?" asks where in any future public service content system is the place for young people themselves as makers and sharers of content? All of the above options should take this into account. By diminishing the power of the commissioning system, it should be possible to envisage a scenario in which young people who might have been YouTube influencers could achieve revenue from the YACF and respect from their audience by producing content which complies with a set of public service rules that should be understood by all young people as result of their education in media literacy and critical thinking.

I doubt questions such as these are in the minds of the DCMS Advisory Panel or Ofcom as we go into the decision-making on the future of public service content in the UK. But they should be. In the medium term, maintaining the BBC and its funding is vital – especially when other public service broadcasters may, despite the success of the Young Audiences Content Fund, be moving away from their obligations.

However, in the long run, the BBC cannot continue to paper over the cracks of the growing audience loss to other services, a loss most prominent in the younger demographics, and a loss it would now be near-impossible to turn around. So, more radical thinking about the role of the BBC, of the regulator, of technology for delivery, especially AI, of the sources and disbursement of funding and the meaning and purpose of public service content – all of these need to be considered now. ☉

OUR WRITERS

Japhet Asher

Japhet is the director of Polarity Reversal Ltd, where he creates IP for a variety of platforms. He also consults with publishing, digital and other media companies to develop ideas, strategies and products. He started out as a writer and documentary maker, then went on to become a partner in the ground breaking animation studio Colossal Pictures, culminating in the TV series he created for MTV and the BBC, 'Liquid Television'.

After 25 years working in the United States, primarily as a television writer/producer and interactive content maker, Japhet returned to the UK and joined the BBC as an executive producer overseeing Children's content development. He was subsequently in charge of digital content for CBBC, where he developed the channel's mobile and app strategy as well as establishing YouTube channels for CBBC and CBeebies. Japhet is also known as a pioneer in augmented reality powered storytelling, combining digital and print to create immersive experiences.

Baroness Floella Benjamin DBE and Julie Elliott MP

Julie Elliott MP and Baroness Floella Benjamin DBE are Co-Chairs of the All-Party Parliamentary Group for Children's Media and the Arts, which was established in 2011 to provide greater awareness of the issues around children's media, arts and culture. It brings together the interests of both audience and industry within a wide cultural, social and educational context to promote first class provision for children.

Jenny Buckland

Jenny is the CEO of the Australian Children's Television Foundation (ACTF). She is a lawyer with extensive experience in the production, financing and international distribution of children's television programmes. She has played a key role in positioning the ACTF as a national children's media and policy hub, and growing the business to become one of the most successful international marketers of children's television programmes.

Greg Childs

Greg Childs is Director of the Children's Media Foundation. He worked for over 25 years at the BBC, mainly as a director, producer and executive producer of children's programmes. He created the first Children's BBC websites and as Head of Children's Digital developed and launched the children's channels, CBBC and CBeebies. Greg left the BBC in 2004 and went on to advise producers on digital, interactive and cross-platform strategies, and broadcasters on channel launches, digital futures and operational management. He was in the launch teams for Teachers TV and the CITV Channel in the UK, and was advisor to the Al Jazeera Children's Channel for three years. He also consulted with the European Broadcasting Union on their Children's and Youth strategy. As Editorial Director of the Children's Media Conference,

Greg has grown this annual event into a gathering of 1,200+ delegates, with over 200 speakers, with spin-off events and activities year-round. He is an associate of the German Akademie für Kindermedien, having spent 15 years as one of the organisation's Heads of Studies.

Frank Cottrell-Boyce

Frank Cottrell-Boyce is a successful British screenwriter whose film credits include 'Welcome to Sarajevo', 'Hilary and Jackie' and '24 Hour Party People'. 'Millions', his debut chidlren's novel, won the 2004 Carnegie Medal and was shortlisted for the Guardian Children's Fiction Award. His second novel, 'Framed', was shortlisted for the 2005 Whitbread Children's Fiction Award and has also been shortlisted for the 2005 Carnegie Medal. His third novel, 'Cosmic', was shortlisted for the Carnegie Medal, the Guardian Children's Fiction Prize and the Roald Dahl Funny Prize. Frank has also written a sensational sequel to the much-loved 'Chitty Chitty Bang Bang' and the heartwarming 'Runaway Robot'.

Cressida Cowell

Waterstones Children's Laureate Cressida Cowell MBE is the number one bestselling author-illustrator of the *How to Train Your Dragon* and *The Wizards of Once* book series. *How to Train Your Dragon* is also an award-winning DreamWorks film franchise. Cressida is a trustee of World Book Day, a patron of Read for Good, an ambassador for the National Literacy Trust and the Woodland Trust, and on the Council of the Society of Authors. She has won many high-profile awards for her books, as well as her work championing literacy. She is an honorary fellow of Keble College, Oxford, and has an honorary doctorate from the University of Brighton.

Nicky Cox MBE and Simona Karabyn

Nicky Cox is founder and editor of children's newspaper 'First News' which reaches 2.6m+ readers a week in more than a third of UK schools. She is also CEO of Fresh Start Media, specialising in making programmes with young people for young people – like Sky TV's 'FYI'. For 13 years, she was editorial director of BBC Worldwide's children's division – contributing BBCWW funds to CBBC shows, and heading up the brand development of BBC assets into magazines, books, audio, toys, games and other products. She is a special adviser to Unicef, patron of the British Citizen Youth Awards and Ambassador of the Global Teacher Prize. She has a quality control panel in her own four children!

Simona Karabyn joined Fresh Start Media in 2019, and has worked primarily as the co-Producer and Programme Editor of weekly Sky News and Sky kids news show, 'FYI', alongside Executive Producer, Chris Rogers. Prior to joining Fresh Start Media, Simona worked as a freelance Television Producer. She brings varied TV genre experience to her role. Beginning her television career in Entertainment, she worked on prime-time shows, (BBC One's 'Strictly Come Dancing' and ITV's 'Britain's Got Talent'), before moving into Factual (Channel 4's award winning 'The Secret Life of 4 & 5 year-olds'), and live studio, Current Affairs and Consumer programmes (BBC One's 'Watchdog's Rogue Traders' and 'The One Show').

John Dale

John worked as an actor and then became a Director at the Royal Court Theatre, London, responsible for young writing. He joined the BBC as a kids' writer/director and then ITV, developing successful television formats, including the 'No 73' Saturday morning show, before going on to write and produce mainstream award-winning adult drama. Pausing briefly to become an academic and gaining a Fellowship for his work on digital communities, he returned to the BBC to help set up the new digital channels and then went to head an innovation unit in BBC Strategy, whilst also being seconded to the Cabinet Office.

John led consultancy teams for new broadcast TV channels in Turkmenistan, Georgia and Zimbabwe. He then decided to stop being a grown-up and created Limetools Ltd., a company that uses John's storytelling and educational experience to build behaviour change tools for areas of organisational high risk, primarily Cyber and Energy Security and Innovation Management. He lives in Bournemouth and still occasionally fire-eats.

Jackie Edwards

Jackie is Head of the BFI Young Audiences Content Fund, and is responsible for the successful implementation of this game-changing UK Government initiative to stimulate the provision of public service content for audiences of 0-18.

Jackie joined the BFI from BBC Children's where she had been the Head of Acquisitions and Independent Animation, responsible for pre-buying and acquiring live-action and animated programming for CBeebies, CBBC and iPlayer. She joined the BBC in 2008 as Content Manager and Executive Producer. Prior to the BBC Jackie was a producer in the Independent Sector. A passionate advocate for public service content, Jackie is living her dream job!

Dr Mai Elshehaly and Professor Mark Mon-Williams

Dr Mai Elshehaly is a Lecturer in Computer Science at the University of Bradford. She holds a PhD and MSc in Computer Science from the Center for Human-Computer Interaction at Virginia Tech, and a BSc in Computer Science from the Suez Canal University. Mai is the Director of the Digital Makers Programme (together with Dr Faisal Mushtaq from the University of Leeds), a cross-sector initiative that is building a scientific approach to the digital upskilling of children and young people in the City of Bradford. She is also the Deputy Director of the Workforce Observatory for the West Yorkshire and Harrogate Integrated Care System. Her primary research interests are in Human-Computer Interaction and Visual Analytics, particularly the human-centred design of visualisation and machine learning algorithms to support big data insights. She is a member of the advisory board for the Wolfson Centre for Applied Health Research, leads the Digital Technologies theme within the Centre for Applied Education Research, and is the University of Bradford lead for the Digital Divide theme within the Child of the North initiative (a large project organised by nine research intensive universities in the North of England, aimed at improving outcomes for children).

Professor Mark Mon-Williams holds a Chair in Cognitive Psychology at the University of Leeds, is Professor of Psychology at the Bradford Institute of Health Research, and Professor of Vision Science at The Norwegian Centre for Vision.

He is also a Turing Fellow at The Alan Turing Institute (the UK's National data analytics and AI Centre). Mark is the Founder Director of the Centre for Immersive Technologies at the University of Leeds – with Immersive Technologies being a major research priority for the University. His work on immersive technologies was headline news around the world in 1994 when he first showed the need to consider human physiology in the design of immersive technology systems. He leads the NHS ARC group responsible for 'Healthy Schools' and is an executive member of the Born in Bradford project (a longitudinal cohort study following the lifelong development of 13,500+ children). His research is funded by a number of organisations including the EPSRC, EEF, MRC and ESRC. He is the lead for the 'Healthy Learning' theme within the UK's 'ActEarly' Prevention Research Programme (funded by a consortium of 20 medical charities led by the UK's Medical Research Council). Mark has several advisory roles including being a Digital Futures Commissioner, being a member of the cross-Whitehall Data Improvement Across Government committee, acting as a scientific adviser to the Social Mobility Commission, and leading a National project on the use of data to identify and support children with vulnerabilities.

Dr Shelley Anne Galpin

Shelley Anne Galpin worked as a teacher in London for several years, before studying for her AHRC-funded PhD at the University of York, where she researched the responses of teenage audiences to the period drama genre. This work will be published in her forthcoming book '*Teenage Audiences and British Period Drama*'. Shelley's work has also been published in *The Journal of British Cinema and Television*, *Studies in European Cinema* and the edited collection *Intercultural Screen Adaptation* (Edinburgh University Press, 2020).

Timandra Harkness

Timandra Harkness writes and presents BBC Radio 4 documentaries, including '*Divided Nation*' and '*Five Knots*', and series '*FutureProofing*' and '*Steelmanning*'. Regular Radio and TV appearances to discuss current affairs, especially issues around technology, include '*Newsnight*', '*Any Questions*', '*Politics Live*' and '*Free Thinking*'.

Her first book, '*Big Data: does size matter?*' was published by Bloomsbury Sigma in 2016 (updated paperback edition 2017).Timandra won the Independent newspaper's column-writing competition with a short piece on goat-borrowing, and has since written for innumerable publications, including *The Times*, *Daily Telegraph*, *BBC Science Focus* and *Unherd*. A Graduate Fellow of the Royal Statistical Society, Timandra writes regularly for their journal, *Significance*.

Patricia Hidalgo

Patricia Hidalgo is Director of Children's & Education at the BBC. She is responsible for developing and implementing creative and editorial strategy for BBC Children's services across all platforms, with a focus on the strategic future direction of media consumption and business models. Patricia also heads up the two most popular networks for children in the UK, CBeebies and CBBC, and leads the BBC's Education department, overseeing all the division's content output including in-house productions, co-productions and acquisitions.

Patricia has a strong industry track record and is behind some of the most successful shows in kids' TV. During her last six years at Turner she was responsible for the production of the multiple award-winning series '*The Amazing World Of Gumball*', as well as the Emile-awarded and Bafta-nominated '*The Heroic Adventures Of The Valiant Prince Ivandoe*'. In 2017 Hidalgo was awarded World Screen's Global Kids Trendsetter award for her outstanding contribution to the kids' media industry. Prior to her role at Turner, Patricia spent 15 years at Disney where she held a number of senior roles in Spain, Italy and the UK.

David Kleeman

Strategist, analyst, author, speaker, connector — David Kleeman has led the children's media industry in developing sustainable, child-friendly practices for 35 years. He began this work as president of the American Centre for Children and Media and is now Senior Vice President of Global Trends for Dubit, a strategy/research consultancy and digital studio.

When he began this work, "children's media" meant television. Today, he is fascinated by, and passionate about, kids' wide range of possibilities for entertainment, engagement, play and learning. David uses research, insights and experience to show that much may change, but children's developmental path and needs remain constant. David is advisory board chair to the international children's TV festival PRIX JEUNESSE, on the board of the Children's Media Association (USA) and the Advisory Board of the Joan Ganz Cooney Centre. He has served as a Senior Fellow of the Fred Rogers Centre and Board Vice President for the National Association for Media Literacy Education.

Wincie Knight

Wincie Knight is VP of Global Inclusion Strategies at ViacomCBS Networks International (VCNI). Fiercely passionate about the notion of diversity being less about filling quotas and more about creating a sense of belonging. She works collaboratively with all of VIMN's Employee Resource Groups in offices in London, Amsterdam, Berlin, Budapest, Madrid, Milan and Warsaw.

Under her strategic guidance, ERGs empower all employees to have a voice as they develop initiatives that positively impact the business and build a sense of community. She played a key role in launching '*ViaYou…Getting To Know You*', an employee survey focused on better understanding workforce demographics, and organised Unconscious Bias and Inclusive Leadership learning opportunities. Furthermore, Wincie Knight has been instrumental in Viacom's participation in Project Diamond and regularly partners internally in articulating VIMN's initiatives to Ofcom.

Anne Longfield OBE

Anne Longfield has spent the last three decades working to improve the life chances of children, particularly the most vulnerable. From March 2015 to February 2021, she was Children's Commissioner for England and previously led a national children's charity.

Anne remains a passionate champion for children, influencing and shaping the national debate and policy agenda for children and their families. She spent many years campaigning for better childcare, often at a time when many saw the issue as obscure or niche. As Children's Commissioner, Anne spent six years championing the rights and interests of children with those in power who make decisions about children's lives, acting as children's 'eyes and ears' in the corridors of power in Whitehall and Westminster.

Emerita Professor Máire Messenger Davies

Máire Messenger Davies is Emerita Professor of Media Studies at Ulster University, and a Visiting Professor at the University of South Wales. She has a BA in English from Trinity College Dublin and, after a journalistic career in local newspapers and national magazines, she obtained a PhD in psychology at the University of East London, studying how audiences learn from television.

She has worked at Boston University and at the University of Pennsylvania in the USA, and later, in the School of Journalism, Media and Cultural Studies, at Cardiff University. She specializes in the study of child media audiences, and is the author of several books including 'Children, Media and Culture' (McGraw Hill/Open University, 2010); 'Dear BBC: Children, Television Storytelling and the Public Sphere' (Cambridge University Press, 2001), 'Television is Good for Your Kids' (Hilary Shipman, (1989, 2002) and, with Roberta Pearson, 'Star Trek and American Television' (University of California Press, 2014.)

Warren Nettleford

Warren Nettleford is an award-winning national TV journalist who's tackled the biggest global news stories covering Europe, Asia and the United States. He's worked for every major UK news broadcaster (BBC, ITV, Channel 4, Channel 5). Covering four General Election campaigns, he's interviewed the last three UK Prime Ministers. Notably he has more recently reported on the Windrush Scandal and the Government's response to the Covid-19 pandemic. In 2021 Warren, alongside his friend and colleague Seth Goolnik, won a Royal Television Society Award - beating the BBC and CNN - for their youth political series 'Need to Know', which was broadcast exclusively online during the 2019 General Election. Warren is from Dudley in the West Midlands.

Dr Jane O'Connor

Dr Jane O'Connor is a Reader in Childhood Studies at Birmingham City University where she co-leads the Cultures in Education research group. She is the author of 'The Cultural Significance of the Child Star' (Routledge, 2008) and co-editor of 'Childhood and Celebrity' (Routledge, 2017). Jane has published extensively in the areas of representations of childhood in the media and young children's use of interactive digital technology. She is currently leading an international project exploring young children's engagement with YouTube Kids. Jane teaches on the MA and EdD in the School of Education and supervises a wide range of PhD projects in the area of Childhood Studies.

Lord David Puttnam

Lord David Puttnam is the Chair of Atticus Education, an online education company founded in 2012 that delivers audio-visual seminars to students all over the world. In addition to this, he is a member of the House of Lords where he pursues an active role in a variety of areas, from educational and environmental issues to digital skills. In 2019, he was appointed to chair a special inquiry committee to investigate the impact of digital technologies on democracy. The committee's findings were published in June 2020. He spent thirty years as an independent producer of award-winning films including 'The Mission', 'The Killing Fields', 'Chariots of Fire', 'Midnight Express', 'Bugsy Malone' and 'Local Hero'. Together these films have won 10 Oscars, 31 BAFTAs, 13 Golden Globes, nine Emmys, four David di Donatellos in Italy and the Palme D'Or at Cannes

Dr. Karl Rawstrone

Dr. Karl Rawstrone is a Senior Lecturer in Media Production and Deputy Head of the Department of Media Production at Bournemouth University. He completed his PhD with the University of the West of England in 2020. His thesis is entitled 'Negotiating Dependence: Independent Television Producers in England'. Karl was a videotape editor at the BBC and Channel 4, working on a great deal of children's content. He was later a director and producer at The Children's Channel. He began teaching in 2000 at a West London secondary school, moved into further education and latterly into higher education. Teaching has been his way of helping young people to make and consume better content.

Sir Phil Redmond

Sir Phil Redmond is a great advocate and ambassador for Liverpool and Merseyside. He was considered innovative throughout his television career at Mersey Television and created a number of ground-breaking drama series including 'Grange Hill', 'Brookside' and 'Hollyoaks'. Through his promotion of arts and culture, he is a driver for positive change across the nation. In 2008 when Liverpool was European Capital of Culture (ECoC) Phil used his high profile to build support for the year-long event, not only within the city itself, but across the UK and internationally. He currently chairs the advisory panel for the UK City of Culture programme.

John Richmond

John Richmond has spent his career working in education and television, both as a teacher and a commissioning editor for schools programming at Channel 4. He helped to set up Children's Television Trust International and was one of the organisers, in 1998, of the second global children's media conference in London. He went on to work at Teachers TV and helped to establish a successful formula that was subsequently adopted in other countries, including the United States, where the Bill and Melinda Gates Foundation established Teaching Channel, where John was Vice-President, Production.

Michael Rosen

A former Children's Laureate and one of the best-known figures in the children's book world, Michael Rosen is renowned for his work as a poet, performer, broadcaster and scriptwriter. As an author and by selecting other writers' works for anthologies he has been involved with over 140 books. He lectures and teaches in universities on children's literature, reading and writing.

Michael is a familiar voice to BBC listeners and is currently presenting 'Word of Mouth', the magazine programme that looks at the English language and the way we use it. He visits schools with his one-man show to enthuse children with his passion for books and poetry. He was one of the first poets to make visits to schools throughout the UK and has also visited schools throughout the world.

Professor Jeanette Steemers

Jeanette Steemers is Professor of Culture, Media and Creative Industries, and Vice Dean of Research in the Faculty of Arts and Humanities at King's College London. A graduate in German and Russian, she completed her PhD on public service broadcasting in West Germany in 1990.

After working for research company, CIT Research, and distributor, HIT Entertainment, she rejoined academia in 1993. Her publications include 'Changing Channels' (1998), 'Selling Television' (2004), 'European Television Industries' (2005 with P. Iosifidis and M. Wheeler), 'Creating Preschool Television' (2010), 'The Media and the State' (2016 with T. Flew and P. Iosifidis), 'European Media in Crisis' (2015 with J. Trappel and B. Thomass), 'Children's TV and Digital Media in the Arab World' (2017 with Naomi Sakr), and 'Screen Media for Arab and European Children' (2019 with Naomi Sakr). She has published widely on distribution, public service broadcasting and the children's media industry. Her work has been funded by the British Academy, the Leverhulme Trust and the Arts and Humanities Research Council.

Ed Vaizey

Ed Vaizey (Lord Vaizey of Didcot) is a member of the House of Lords, appointed in 2020, and sits on the Communications and Media Committee. He was the Member of Parliament for Wantage between 2005 and 2019. He served as the UK Government Culture and Digital Minister from 2010-16, and is the longest-serving minister in that role. He was appointed a Privy Councillor in 2016.

In his role as digital minister, Ed was responsible for the roll out of the successful rural broadband programme to more than 4 million homes, and the introduction of 4G, and tax credits for film, television, animation and video games, which have helped make the creative industries the fastest growing part of the UK economy. In addition, he played a key role in putting coding in the national curriculum for schools, and in attracting inward investment to the UK tech economy. Ed also helped persuade Lucas Films to make the new 'Star Wars' in the UK, and received an on-screen credit in the first film of the series. He currently serves as a trustee of the National Youth Theatre, the Documentary Society and London Music Masters, and is a patron of Kids in Museums.

Tom Van Waveren

Tom van Waveren began his career in animation at Nelvana in 1996 as Director of its London office. In 1999, Tom moved to Copenhagen to head up Egmont Imagination as its President where he was involved in the production of over 100 hours of animation, including '*Paz*', '*Rex the Runt*', '*Little People*' and '*Hamilton Mattress*', and the distribution of '*Lizzie McGuire*'.

Tom started his own company Hoek, Line & Thinker in 2004 and merged his pipeline of projects with CAKE in 2006. He was responsible for scouting, development and the executive production of all CAKE content.

Tom was the CEO and Creative Director at CAKE from 2006 through to 2021. He has been nominated three times for a daytime Emmy (still waiting for that win) and oversaw a development slate of over 20 properties from pre-school to animation for 6-12 years, as well as all CAKE's current productions, which have included over the years, '*Skunk Fu!*', '*Angelo Rules*', '*Oscar's Oasis*', '*Space Chickens in Space*', '*Mush Mush and the Mushables*', '*Mama K's Team 4*', and '*Angry Birds: Summer Madness*'.

Tom is currently a Vice-Chair of Animation in Europe, where he is working to improve support for the European animation industry.

Anne Wood CBE

In 1984 Anne Wood founded Ragdoll Productions, whose work is loved by children around the world. Since then, Ragdoll has produced more than 1,500 programmes aimed at the youngest viewers, including a number of award-winning shows, particularly the hugely successful '*Teletubbies*' and '*In the Night Garden*'. Ragdoll won the BAFTA Children's Award for Independent Production Company 2008.

Anne was born in County Durham and qualified as a secondary school teacher. One of her early missions was to encourage children to read. After founding the '*Books for Your Children*' magazine and setting-up the Federation of Children's Book Groups, Anne became a sought-after consultant embracing book publishing, radio and television. She took the leap into independent TV production when she founded Ragdoll Productions, now known as an innovative content provider.

Peter York and Emeritus Professor Patrick Barwise

Peter York is a 'capitalist tool' by background, as a market researcher (like Paddy Barwise a Patron of the Market Research Society) and management consultant. In parallel he is a social commentator, journalist, occasional TV presenter and author of eleven books, ranging from the best-selling '*Official Sloane Ranger Handbook*' to '*Authenticity is a Con*', an attack on the cult of authenticity. Patrick Barwise is emeritus professor of management and marketing at London Business School and an expert on marketing and media, specialising in customer-focused strategy and execution, marketing leadership, brands, advertising, media, and broadcasting policy.

Their book '*The War Against the BBC*' was published by Penguin in November 2020 https://www.penguin.co.uk/books/311/311439/the-war-against-the-bbc/9780141989402.html

OUR CHILDREN'S FUTURE:
JOIN THE DEBATE

thechildrensmediafoundation.org/public-service-media-report

The Children's Media
FOUNDATION

www.ingramcontent.com/pod-product-compliance
Lightning Source LLC
Chambersburg PA
CBHW061012030426
42336CB00028B/3453